Wayne Bank and Trust Co.
SINCE 1882

Seven Generations in Wayne County!

When Samuel Boyd, a revolutionary soldier, settled near Jacksonburg in Wayne County in 1811 he did not realize that his grandson would establish the Western Wayne Bank in 1882, which was the predecessor to the present Wayne Bank and Trust Company.

Since August 1882, we have faithfully served our community as a locally owned and independent community bank.

In 1997 Wayne Bank and Trust Company celebrated its 115th anniversary as the oldest family owned bank in Indiana.

Wayne Bank is proud to sponsor this limited edition of *A Pictorial History of Wayne County Indiana* in appreciation of the continuing trust placed in us by the people of our area. We dedicate this book to all of our friends who have made our success possible.

A special thanks to Carolyn Lafever for her timeless efforts in making this book the beautiful tribute that it is.

Proceeds from the sale of this book will benefit the Wayne County Historical Museum one of Wayne County's finest cultural and educational institutions.

Alonzo Hernly Boyd Jr.
President

Drawings by Jack Phelps

Motion pictures being taken of the original Light Inspection Car, circa 1930s, first built in 1894 in Hagerstown. The company became the Perfect Circle Corporation with factories in Richmond and Hagerstown.

A Pictorial History of
Wayne County, Indiana

By Carolyn Lafever

To Clare & Charlene,
Enjoy your trip through
Wayne County.

Carolyn Lafever

THE
DONNING COMPANY
PUBLISHERS

The Donning Company/Publishers
184 Business Park Drive Suite 106
Virginia Beach, VA 23462

Steve Mull, General Manager
Ed Williams, Project Director
Paula A. Ridge, Project Research Coordinator
Dawn V. Kofroth, Assistant General Manager
Sally C. Davis, Associate Editor
Paul C. Gualdoni Jr., Graphic Designer
Teri S. Arnold, Senior Marketing Coordinator

Library of Congress Cataloging-in-Publication Data

Lafever, Carolyn
      A pictorial history of Wayne County, Indiana/by Carolyn Lafever.
              p.   cm.
      Includes bibliographical references and index.
      ISBN 1-57864-029-6 (alk. paper)
      1. Wayne County (Ind.)—History—Pictorial works.   I. Title.
F532.W5L34   1998
977.2'63—dc21   98–10951
                                            CIP

Printed in the United States of America

Contents

Opening of the State Theater on Main Street, Richmond. "Richmond's Big Event, May 10, 1941." Herbie Day and orchestra performed on stage and the movie starred Charlie Chaplin.

Preface

Wayne County was one of the first counties formed in the Indiana Territory. Its early political influence helped persuade Indiana to be free of slavery when it became the nineteenth state in 1816. The men and women who settled Wayne County brought strong religious convictions and a willingness to work hard, turning them toward building one of Indiana's most prosperous areas.

The photographs we chose from the hundreds available, show ordinary people going about their work. Others depict homes, historical and cultural sites and business. Every picture tells a story and shows how important each of us are in living the history of our own places.

It is our desire to encourage the continued writing of family and community history and the preservation of pictures. For over a century and a half we have been able to capture moments in time with the camera. Time spent in caring for old documents and labeling pictures will benefit future generations.

Wooden dam, circa 1903, on Nettle Creek which furnished water power for the old Test Woolen Mill. The mill was in Dalton Township and was located on the Jefferson/Dalton line, on the Franklin road. After 1899 it was Parsons' Slaughter House.

Acknowledgments

The history of Wayne County has been well documented in five large books, beginning with Andrew W. Young's *History of Wayne County* in 1872. It was followed by the *History of Wayne County* by the Inter-State Publishing Company in 1884 and by *Memoirs of Wayne County and the City of Richmond* by Henry C. Fox in 1912. Several books have been written about the towns in the county. The Palladium-Item newspaper has published several anniversary editions which included much county history. Their history columns by Luther Feeger and others have recorded history found in no other places.

It was a coincidence that the Wayne County Historical Museum began thinking about the need for a new county history at the same time Wayne Bank and Trust Company indicated interest in this type of project. The Donning Company/Publishers brought the two together and with the selection of an author, the project was launched in December of 1996.

Without the help of the generous people of Wayne County it would have been very difficult to find the interesting pictures and information. Jack Phelps provided drawings, photographs and books. Wayne Bank's picture collection was a great help with Jackson Township. Wayne County Historical Museum's archives and picture collection was invaluable. Special help and photographs were given by Inezetta Stiver for Center Township, Phyllis Mattheis for Jackson, Lewis Farmer for Clay, Marilyn Kelley for Boston, Libby Rusk for Abington, Joe and Verna Toney for Boston. Saundra Jackson of the Levi Coffin House helped with New Garden and Franklin. Ed Smith helped with research for Wayne Township. Several other residents of the townships, whose names are with the illustrations, provided pictures, documents, genealogy, gave interviews and helped proofread. Lois and Eric Herzog, Wanda Campbell, Luther Parsons, Marcia and Malcolm Jeffers also were proofreaders.

Each of the libraries in the county, Morrison-Reeves in Richmond, the Cambridge City Library, Dublin Library, Hagerstown Library and the Centerville Library, provided pictures and research facilities. I found many interesting things in the Indiana Room at the Anderson Public Library. The files of Wayne County genealogist, Beverly Yount, had been placed in the Indiana Room.

Preparing the pictures was one of the most demanding tasks. My husband, Edward, photographed many of the copies and toured the county with me, taking more photographs. Jim Stevenson of Stevenson's Photography made wonderful prints of our pictures and provided some of his own. The Photo-Copy Center in Richmond made good copies and gave excellent and quick service.

The most help with this project came from friends and family who gave encouragement. This is not the work of a single author, but a joint effort of many people who cared and took time to help. My thanks to you all.

Wayne County
Indiana

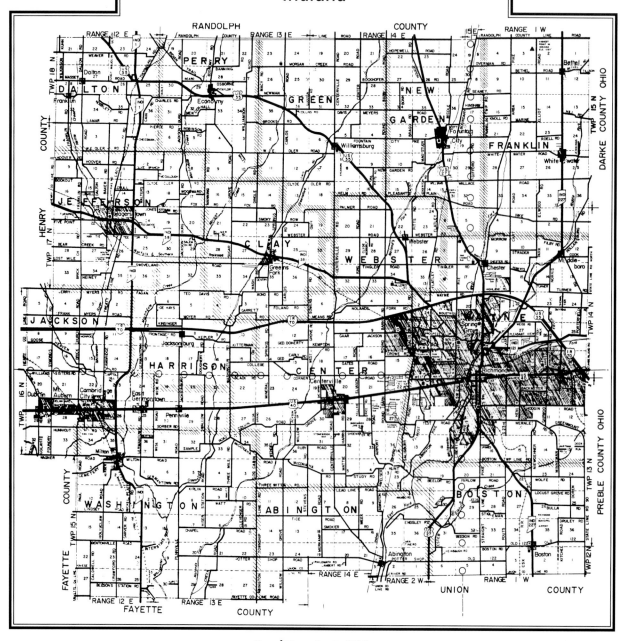

Map of Wayne County, 1977.

Introduction

For whom was Wayne County named? Who were its first settlers? How many courthouses has the county had? Those questions—and hundreds more—are answered in a new pictorial history of Wayne County written by Dalton Township resident Carolyn Lafever.

This is the first history of Wayne County published since 1912. It comes just three years after the publication of a pictorial history of Richmond written by the late Gertrude Ward. The two volumes are like bookends, embracing between them the rich history of the county and the city which serves as the county seat.

There has been a need for a new county history since the previous five volumes were primarily about the earlier years of the nineteenth century. A new book was needed to cover the twentieth century. The result is 192 pages filled with written history, illustrated with more than 270 pictures.

The book tells the story of a county which once was Indiana's most prosperous and populous. From its nineteenth century roots evolved the vigorous county now readying for the twenty-first century. The pictures range from the blockhouses (forts) of the earliest years to structures of more recent vintage; from blacksmith shops to churches; from ordinary citizens to a portrait of Oliver P. Morton, Indiana's Civil War governor, a native of Wayne County.

The book has fourteen chapters. The first chapter deals with early Wayne County and how it developed. The second chapter, appropriately titled "A Century of Progress," recounts in pictures and words the development of the county in the twentieth century. The final chapters cover Wayne County's fifteen townships. On the lead page of each township section is a small Wayne County map with the township outlined in its proper place. Again, words and pictures report the story of each township.

The pictorial history was completed after a year's effort which included hundreds of interviews, hundreds of miles traveled, hundreds of pictures located and hundreds of hours of research.

The author's interest in history was ignited in her high school years and continued at Ball State University. She is a native of neighboring Randolph County but has lived near Hagerstown for three decades. This is not her first venture into original research. Author Lafever has written other books and magazine articles about Wayne County history, but this has been her most ambitious project.

The Pictorial History of Wayne County is designed to be a place for young people to start their own research. Those who have lived the history will find it well written, a trustworthy book and valuable for its presentation of the rich history of Wayne County, Indiana.

Dick Reynolds

Clearing the Land from a drawing by R. E. Robinson in "American Agriculture," April, 1880. Courtesy Wayne County Historical Museum

Chapter 1

Wayne County – The Early Years

Wayne County, situated in east central Indiana at the Ohio state line, was formed in 1810. Its political history began in 1787 when an ordinance was passed by the Continental Congress forming the Northwest Territory. The lands were given by New York, Virginia, Connecticut and Massachusetts to the General Government to help raise funds to pay the Revolutionary War debt. The North West Territory included lands from which the states of Ohio, Indiana, Illinois, Michigan and Wisconsin were formed.

Arthur St. Clair was elected governor of the territory in 1787. He was succeeded by William Henry Harrison who became governor of the Indiana Territory in 1800 when the Northwest Territory was divided. The eastern division, Ohio, was admitted as a state in 1802. The western division, the Indiana Territory, was admitted to statehood in 1816. From 1802 to 1805, Harrison negotiated treaties with the Indian tribes. In 1803 there were five counties in the Indiana Territory; Dearborn, Clark, Knox, St. Clair and Randolph. There had been a sixth county, the old Wayne county which covered much of Michigan. In 1805 the territory of Michigan was formed and the old Wayne County was eliminated. Indiana Territory was further divided in 1809 by establishing Illinois which left Indiana with nearly the same boundaries of today.

In 1810 a new Wayne County was formed, its name honoring the hero of the American Revolution and many Indian wars, General Anthony Wayne. Although the area was now open to settlers it was not free of danger. The territory was still the home of American Indians and at one time the Whitewater Valley was the hunting ground of the "Six Nations." This valu-

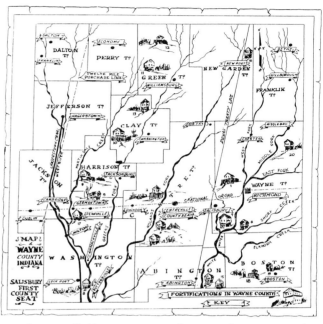

Fortifications or blockhouses in Wayne Co. during War of 1812. Courtesy of Wayne County Museum

John Finley, Editor of the *Richmond Palladium*, fixed the name "Hoosier" on Indiana with his poem, "The Hoosier Nest" which appeared in the *Indianapolis Journal*, January 1, 1833. Finley, Indiana's first poet, gave respectability to the nickname "Hoosier" with his poetic picture of Indiana pioneer life. Before it had been used in a derogatory sense for the primitive lifestyle of Indiana settlers.

A Pictorial History of Wayne County, Indiana

Salisbury, 1812, a rare old newspaper print. In 1816 Salisbury had thirty-five houses, two stores, two taverns and the public buildings. Courtesy of Jack Phelps. Computer enhancement by Max Wood

Wayne County's first courthouse, erected in Salisbury, 1811. It is believed to be the oldest log courthouse in the old Northwest Territory. It is located in Centerville. Courtesy of Wayne County Museum

able common hunting ground was threatened by the white settlers. Hostilities erupted with the Indians in 1811–1812. Settlers in the Whitewater Valley were able to do little more than protect themselves and provide for their necessities. Although most of the battles were fought in other parts of the state, blockhouses or forts were built in Wayne County. By 1814 most of the hostilities had ended, treaties were signed and the little homesteads in the wilderness could again clear lands and plant crops. Most of the Indians had left Wayne County by 1825.

The discovery of the Whitewater Valley in 1804 has been credited to Joseph Wasson, a Revolutionary soldier, and Judge Peter Fleming, both from Kentucky. Richard Rue and George Holman came through the area and entered a claim in Cincinnati the same year. In 1805, Richard Rue, George Holman, Thomas McCoy, Joseph Cox and William Blunt brought their families from Kentucky. According to Sanford C.

Cox, son of Joseph Cox, the party made their settlement on Short Creek about two miles southeast of Richmond. In the spring of 1806, they were visited by David Hoover's party.

David Hoover led a group of Quakers, also called Friends, from North Carolina to the area. They founded the Whitewater settlement of Friends, which would later become Richmond, Indiana. Quakers were opposed to slavery which made them unpopular in the slave states of the South. Their search for a "promised land" led them to the Indiana Territory where they could practice their faith and be free of persecution. The dense forests, abundant water supply and rich virgin soil enticed many Quakers to come to Wayne County.

In 1810 three new counties were formed, Franklin, Jefferson, and a new Wayne in the Upper Whitewater Valley. Richmond or Cox's Settlement as it was then called, was the only village in Wayne County. But it was too far removed from the cen-

The old brick courthouse (No. 4) in Centerville. When Wayne County seat was moved to Richmond, the building was used by the Hoosier Organ Co., circa 1875. It was ravaged by fire in 1914. Courtesy of Inezetta Stiver

ter of the county to qualify for the seat of justice. In 1810, county commissioners were appointed to serve in various capacities, including "Overseers of the Poor" and "Fence Viewers." They were also to "fix the county seat near the geographical center" of the county. A site was chosen north of Centerville, but the land had not yet been offered for sale by the Federal Government. New commissioners were appointed and they selected a location west of Richmond. The new village, a property of sixty-five acres in Wayne Township, was named

Salisbury. According to the description on its plat: "The town of Salisbury stands on a beautiful site of the waters of Clear Creek . . . we flatter ourselves that in a few years, Art with her sister Industry, will convert it from a forest to a flourishing inland Town. Several gentlemen of property have purchased lots, both in the mercantile and mechanical line, which will greatly enhance its importance."

...cated for settlement.
DANIEL CLARK, *Adm'r*.
August 21, 1849. 35-tf

TO TRAVELLERS!!

CINCINNATI OMNIBUS LINE,
Via Boston, Fair Haven, Morning Sun, and
Dartown, RESUMED!!!
THE WESTERN STAGE COMPANY,

RESPECTFULLY inform the travelling public of RICHMOND and surrounding country, that their **Daily Line of Omnibusses,** which was temporarily suspended on account of the prevalence of the Cholera, is again running between *Richmond and Cincinnati.* Those wishing a safe and speedy conveyance to the city, will find it in this line. Leaves Richmond at 7 o'clock, each morning. Leaves Cincinnati same time.
☞Time of running through—Nine Hours.
For seats apply at the office of the Company,

Stage Coach advertisement from an 1849 Richmond paper. The state coach line from Richmond to Cincinnati was temporarily suspended due to a cholera epidemic which nearly wiped out Boston, Indiana. Courtesy of Wayne County Museum

Salisbury became the seat of justice in 1811, the place where county business is carried on and where the courthouse and county officials are situated. In 1811, the courthouse was built of logs and the second was constructed of brick in 1815. Salisbury was the first incorporated town in Wayne County.

In 1816 Indiana became the 19th state to enter the Union. Four villages had been platted in Wayne County; Salisbury 1811, Jacksonburg, 1814, Centerville 1814 and Richmond 1816. Wayne County had six townships; Harrison,

Jackson, New Garden, Perry, Wayne and Washington. Even before Indiana became a state Salisbury, being the county seat, was denounced by those who recognized it was not the center of the county. Centerville, more centrally located, worked to have the county seat moved there. A removal act for the county seat to be moved to Centerville was passed by the State Legislature in 1816. Salisbury refused to give it up and it took two years for Centerville to wrestle the seat of justice from Salisbury. In 1818 a log courthouse (No. 3) was built in Centerville.

A brick courthouse (No. 4) was built in 1845 and was used until 1873. Although Centerville prospered during the years it was the county seat, Richmond grew much larger. In

Staff and visitors in front of Earlham Hall, circa 1862. It began in 1847 as the Friends Boarding School and became Earlham College in 1859. Courtesy of Earlham College Archives

A shipping order from the Whitewater Canal Basin, Cincinnati, to deliver goods to the port of Hagerstown, 1852. Courtesy of Wayne County Museum

1840 Richmond was designated a city and recognized as one of the state's leading industrial and marketing centers. By the 1870s railroads entered it from five directions and there were many successful industries. In 1872 a petition signed by a majority of county citizens was presented to the Commissioners urging a move of the county seat to Richmond. Centerville filed a remonstrance, but the petition was granted. Contracts were let out for a Richmond Courthouse (No. 5) and jail at a cost of $22,700 and Richmond became the county seat in 1873. In 1893 the last Courthouse (No. 6) was built in Richmond. The courthouse annex was built across the street in 1977.

The first wealth and prosperity of Wayne County came from homestead farms. The soil was especially suited to corn, wheat, rye, barley and oats. Hogs, cattle, sheep, horses and chickens were the principle animals raised. Various types of business and industry were quickly established to supply the needs of the pioneers. The Whitewater River is considered the fastest running river in Indiana and there is a drop of elevation from 1,257 feet in Franklin Township to 790 feet at Abington. Because of the many waterways and

A Pictorial History of Wayne County, Indiana

The Vinton House, 1918, located on Main Street in Cambridge City. In 1849 Vinton purchased the hotel naming it the Vinton House. Travelers by stage, canal boat, train, electric car and automobile found shelter there. Vinton and his daughters operated it until about 1919. Courtesy of Jack Phelps

the speed of the water, mills became an important industry in Wayne County. The excellent water power was harnessed for flour mills, grist mills, oil mills, saw mills, fulling mills and woolen mills. According to William Creitz, owner of the Imperial Mill at Cambridge City in 1912, it is a fact of history that there was only one county in the United States with more mills, the county which contains Rochester, New York. According to a paper prepared by William O. Wissler in 1912 there were one hundred sixty-six mill sites in Wayne County.

Transporting products to market became a problem for the pioneers. The fertile farms produced an abundance of crops and animals. The first roads were narrow trails, often muddy and hard to travel. Goods were carried on pack animals or in wagons. Waterways were used whenever possible. Hogs were driven in herds to Cincinnati and it took at least a week to reach the market. In 1803 Congress agreed to build a road over the Allegheny mountains, a grand National Road to connect the Eastern States to the Western Territory. It took from 1806 to 1824 to complete the one hundred thirty-five mile section of the National Road from Cumberland to the Ohio River.

Internal improvements was the leading political theme when Indiana became a state in 1816. After much controversy and delay, the new road was built through Wayne County during the

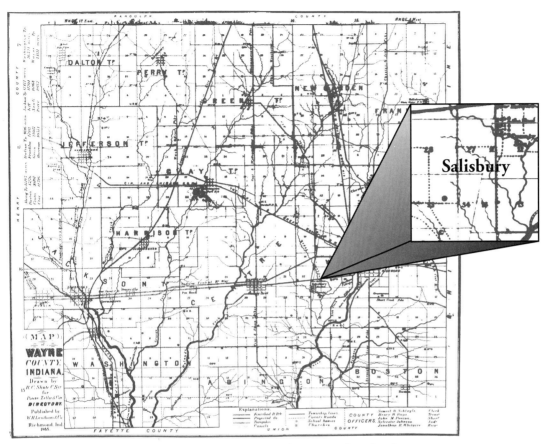

Map of Wayne County, 1865. There were fourteen townships since Webster was not formed until 1870. This is the only county map showing Salisbury. Courtesy of Inezetta Stiver

years of 1835–1837. Hundreds of people passed along the National Road on their journey west. They came on horse back, in oxen-pulled covered wagons, by stage coach and on foot. This road was one of the most important internal improvements made by the Federal Government for its citizens.

Early settlements in Indiana were made along streams and waterways. Farms, villages and towns away from waterways needed better ways to travel and transport their goods. In 1818, Indiana's Governor Jennings declared that roads and canals were needed for commercial transactions connected with the exports and imports of the country. In January, 1836 the Indiana legislature passed the Internal Improvement Bill which appropriated $10,000,000 for canals, roads and

railroads. Wayne County was to benefit by the building of the Whitewater Canal from Hagerstown to Cincinnati.

There was tremendous enthusiasm for the canal and the work commenced. The canal opened in June, 1839 from Lawrenceburg to Brookville. The cost of the project exceeded one million dollars and tolls amounted to just under $10,000. The debt from the improvement projects was a great burden for Indiana taxpayers and finally bankrupt the state. A private company, The Whitewater Valley Canal Company, was formed to build the canal from Brookville to the National Road. It was completed to Cambridge City in October, 1845.

The people of Hagerstown wanted the canal finished as planned so they organized the

A Pictorial History of Wayne County, Indiana

Indiana's Civil War Governor Oliver Morton, 1861–1865, a native of Wayne County. This 1864 painting by Richmond artist Marcus Mote is the only known time Morton sat for a portrait. Other pictures of him are photographs. Courtesy of Richmond Art Museum

The first courthouse built in Richmond (No. 5) was used from 1873 until 1893, when the new courthouse was built beside it. Courtesy of Wayne County Museum

Hagerstown Canal Company. The last eight miles of the canal from Cambridge City to Hagerstown was opened in 1847. Towns along the canal became shipping points and people from all over east central Indiana brought their goods to the canal ports. Iron works, pork packing plants, mills and other industry grew along its path. New streets were laid out in the towns and the population increased. But the canal boom was not to last. In 1847 a flood south of Connersville caused extensive damage. Repairs were barely finished when a series of floods damaged the canal and the company went out of business in the 1850s. The upper canal operated on a limited basis for a few more years.

With the canal companies bankrupt, the state legislature in 1863 passed an enabling act to allow the Whitewater Valley Railroad to purchase the towpath of the canal but not to interfere with water power still in use. Although fortunes were lost and hopes shattered, the construction of the canal encouraged population growth, new manufacturing and helped the farmers thrive. Its benefit to the state and to Wayne County cannot be measured.

Wayne County of the 1840s and 1850s was a hotbed of anti-slavery sentiment. In 1838 Quakers or Friends at Newport (Fountain City) decided to organize an Anti-Slavery Library Society to distribute literature on the subject of anti-slavery. Levi Coffin was appointed to obtain the supplies. At Milton, a group of Friends formed the State Anti-Slavery Society of Indiana. For some time many residents of Wayne County, including Quakers, Methodist, Baptist and other religious persuasions had refused to purchase goods made by slaves. In 1841 the newspaper *Protectionist* and 1843 the *Free Labor Advocate* were established.

M. C. Henley Bicycle Works, N. 16th St., Richmond, circa 1886. Henley began making roller skates and soon added bicycles. The business lasted from 1880 to 1941. Courtesy of Wayne County Museum

The purpose was to awaken the slave-holding states and to point up how liberty and slavery are diametrically opposed to each other.

Not everyone agreed. Churches were split over the issue and many refused to support the efforts of the anti-slavery groups. Those opposed to slavery spoke out, refused to purchase goods not made by free labor, and began to help escaped slaves. Newport became an important stop on the "Underground Railroad" and Levi Coffin with the help of supporters became known as its president or conductor. It is estimated that while at Newport and Cincinnati, Coffin helped over 3,000 fugitive slaves to their freedom.

By virtue of the National Road passing through, Wayne County became the most prosperous county in the state. In 1848 Wayne County had the largest population of any county in Indiana. The tax paid by Wayne County annually exceeded that paid by fourteen of the smaller counties, according to the Indiana Gazetteer of 1850. About three-fifths of the county was in cultivation. A great variety of machinery and farming equipment was produced at Richmond and other places which helped supply the neighboring counties. Mention was also made of the high value Wayne County people placed on education. There were about 100 school districts in the

A Pictorial History of Wayne County, Indiana

View of tracks at the Richmond's railroad yard, 1898. The Old Union Station on the left was used from 1872–1902. Courtesy of Wayne County Museum

An outdoor barbershop in Franklin, Dalton Township. Often more socializing went on than hair cutting. Circa 1890. Courtesy of Letha Goodwin

county, each having a school house. The Friends Boarding School (Earlham) at Richmond, the Richmond Whitewater School, the Whitewater Female College and Whitewater Academy at Centerville were listed.

Railroads came to Wayne County and the first train entered Richmond in 1853. From that time Wayne County lost its edge for being the most prosperous county as other parts of Indiana were opened for manufacturing opportunities and population growth. The railroads caused some county towns to prosper and others to decline, depending on whether a railroad passed through. With more convenient shipping and lowered costs, farmers and manufacturers were able to produce goods for a growing market.

In 1861 Indiana elected its first Indiana-born Governor, Oliver P. Morton. Born in Salisbury (1823) Morton was raised and educated in Centerville. He was elected lieutenant-governor with Henry S. Lane as governor. The plan was, if elected, Lane would become a United States Senator and Morton step in as governor. The first official act of Governor Morton was to send a message to President Lincoln agreeing to send 10,000 men "for the defense of the Nation and to uphold the authority of the Government..." He served as Indiana's Civil War Governor 1861- 65.

Officers and enlisted men from Wayne County served with honor and distinctions. Among the best known are General Solomon Meredith of Cambridge City who led the Nineteenth of Indiana, one of four regiments to make up the famous Iron Brigade. James Prichett of Centerville served as a naval commander of two ironclad ships and was honored many years later by having a destroyer, the USS Prichett, named after him in 1943.

In the 1880s and 90s, manufacturing grew steadily along with new farming techniques. Wayne County led in the manufacture of farm equipment. Telephones connected neighbors. New lighting systems were introduced to light homes and streets of the towns when natural gas was discovered in Wayne County. Turnpike roads were being taken over by the county in the 1890s. Schools began consolidating and high schools were built in several school districts. Cambridge City was among the first to provide for the education of colored children when they built a separate school for them in 1876-77. They were fully incorporated into the school system in 1885.

Residents of Wayne County worked hard to build a prosperous county. It was first in Indiana for many years in population and wealth. The industrious, well established people were ready to turn the calendar page into a new century of progress.

Building the interurban tracks near Heiser station, west of Centerville. Passenger trains ran four times daily, two in each direction. Circa 1902–1903.
Courtesy of Inezetta Stiver

Chapter 2

A Century of Progress

Wayne County residents looked forward to even more opportunities in 1900. Railroads had made great improvements in the ability to travel and to ship goods. The factories of Richmond, Cambridge City and Hagerstown were producing all types of goods and employing hundreds of workers. Shortly after the turn of the century Richmond industrialists started designing and producing "horseless carriages."

But before automobiles could take over roads, interurban transportation came into the county. The first freight and passenger service from Richmond to Centerville began in November, 1902. The first car trip from Richmond to Indianapolis was in June, 1903 and soon after to Dayton. Electric interurbans owed their popularity to the frequency, speed and low cost of their service, compared with similar services by railroads. The company which built Wayne County's first interurban was the Richmond Street and Interurban Railway Co. It was sold to the Terre Haute, Indianapolis and Eastern Traction Co. in 1908, helping Richmond become part of a statewide network of lines.

Interurban transportation reached its peak in 1925 and shortly after began a downhill slide. The decline of the interurban systems was due to the quicker and more convenient service of automobiles, trucks, buses and finally the airplane. Automobiles were being improved along with the growth of the interurban. Wayne County was an early leader in production of the automobile. There were fourteen automobile makers in Richmond. All but one were short-lived. Wayne Works Corporation continued to make school busses until it was sold to the Carpenter Manufacturing Co.

Wayne County Court House (no. 6), 1900. Courtesy of Jim Stevenson

Twelve high schools competed for honors in the Richmond Sectional Basketball Tournament held from 1915 to 1962. From 1962 there were only five teams from Wayne County. In 1997 class basketball tournaments were established based on student enrollment. Remaining five are in bold type.

Boston

Cambridge City

Centerville

Economy

Fountain City

Greens Fork

Hagerstown

Milton

Richmond

Webster

Whitewater

Williamsburg

Citizens Telephone Office, Cambridge City, 1904. Courtesy of Wayne Bank

More and improved railroads were built through the county in the early 1900s. Webster, Williamsburg and Economy benefited from the Richmond to Muncie line in 1901, which eventually became the Chesapeake and Ohio (C & O) line. The Pennsylvania Railroad elevated the tracks through Cambridge City and the improvement of that line helped the towns from Richmond to Dublin.

Agricultural implements had improved along with the economy. Farm families were no longer isolated since the coming of good roads, better transportation and telephones. Whatever was needed could be purchased at the small towns or it could be shipped in from Richmond or Indianapolis. Most people were optimistic about the future until war was declared in Europe in 1914. President Woodrow Wilson declared that the United States would remain neutral. But by 1917 the loss of American life by German attacks against passenger ships could no longer be ignored. Congress declared war on April 6, 1917.

In July 1917, men came to look for places between Dayton and Indianapolis to locate

Stone train working on U.S. 27 through Chester, early 1900s. The crushed stone was put down on a damp surface and pressed into it. This is called a "macadamized" road. Courtesy of Jack Phelps

Aviation stations for government use of airplanes being built at Dayton. The straight line of the National Road would be the guide for training flights. Cambridge City's old fairground was selected as one of the stations. Lamps for the airplane lighthouse were put in place in November. This was the first light tower to be ready in Wayne County and possibly the whole route. In August 1918, five airplanes landed at the former fairgrounds and several thousand people gathered to get their first look at "live airplanes."

For the United States the war lasted less than two years, but it was deeply felt by everyone. Manufacturing shifted to war production, such as Bertsch & Co of Cambridge City. It was one of seven founderies in the U.S. to have the capability to make large castings necessary to con-

The front page of the Richmond Palladium announcing the end of World War I. Courtesy of Wayne County Museum

struct government emergency fleet engines. When the war ended on November 14, 1918, every town celebrated by setting great fires of wood and tar barrels. Turpentine balls were thrown in the air in lieu of fireworks. Bells were rung, parades held, speeches and martial music filled the air. The war was over.

In the wake of relief from the horrors of war, events moved quickly for Wayne County. Automobiles were taking over the roads and by 1919 there were no more tollroads in Wayne County. Steam and gasoline engines had replaced water power and horse power. Many of the small towns had electricity and by the mid-1920s all of them would have it. Farmers were not left behind in the new technology. They had access to acetylene light plants and by 1918 many farmers had Delco-Light and other battery powered plants to provide electricity. The 1920s brought improved roads to Wayne County and many farmers

The equipment for WOZ was the best available when the Richmond Palladium went on the air in 1921. Its broadcast range was a radius of thirty miles. It lasted about two years. Photo by Ed Lafever

A Richmond made Davis airplane taking off from the airfield east of Centerville. Drawing by Jack Phelps

owned automobiles. But most of the farming was still done with work horses. For less prosperous families, old Dobbin still pulled the buggy.

Farmers had realized after the war that they must take the lead in promoting their business. The Wayne County Farm Bureau was organized in 1920. They began to promote cooperative companies such as the Wayne County Produce Association and the Richmond Milk Producers association. They promoted better seed, better farming techniques and better ways to ship livestock directly to market. From this improved communication and farmer education came cooperative elevators and stockyards. In the 1930s Farm Bureaus promoted the Rural

Electrification project (REMC) to bring electricity to all rural areas in the county. In 1921 a new communication link, Palladium's radio station WOZ went on the air. It began to broadcast market reports and programs, another boost to farming business.

In 1919, Claude E. Berry established the first Wayne County airport on U.S. 27 north of Spring Grove (Richmond). He purchased land in 1920 near Centerville to be used as a test field for Davis airplanes which were built in Richmond. John Nixon bought the airfield and Wilfred Jessup added his acreage of the old Centerville fairgrounds. This became the Nixon Airport. In 1942 the airport closed after a decision was made

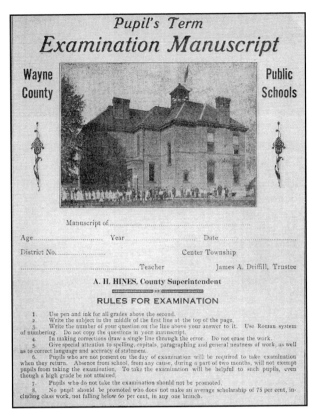

Pupil's Term
Examination Manuscript

Wayne County — Public Schools

An Examination Manuscript cover provided by the Wayne County School Superintendent, circa 1930s. Pupils who did not achieve an average of 75 percent including classwork, were not to be promoted. Courtesy of Inezetta Stiver

Well known Richmond and Wayne County artists. Front row, l-r: Unknown boy, Fred Pearce of Williamsburg, Eddie Forkner. Second, l-r: John E. Bundy, Mrs. M. F. Johnson (founder of the Richmond Art Society), Esther Griffin White. Back row, l-r: Mr. Holly, Mac Nordyke, Al Gregg, Frank Giriadin. Courtesy of Richmond Art Musuem

that it could not be used by the Civil Air Patrol. In 1943 Richmond proposed to purchase land in Boston Township for a municipal airport. The new airport was dedicated July 4–5, 1945.

Nearly all the county townships built new school facilities in the 1920s. There had been a Wayne County school superintendent since 1873. Richmond, Hagerstown and Cambridge City had their own superintendents which left nine county schools for the Wayne County superintendent to oversee. Students were expected to perform well and judged by their hard work and test scores.

The stock market crash of 1929 effected everyone. The 1930s and 1940s were years of head-cracking labor disputes. Politics were changing and the New Deal helped raise the hopes of the desperate. Some companies were able to survive better than others. The Perfect

Circle Company of Hagerstown helped many employees by giving them short work weeks so they could have a paycheck. People lost their jobs and homes, but it brought about a new sense of appreciation for what they had and the ability to "tighten their belts."

The experience of the depression helped people manage the shortages of the second World War which came in 1940. Hundreds of young men and women from Wayne County served in the military, the Red Cross and worked in factories. Manufacturing was shifted to war production. Everything which was not necessary was put on hold. The roads suffered from materials to repair them. There were no new farm implements and the faithful horse was put back to work. The war ended in 1945.

A Pictorial History of Wayne County, Indiana

Army and Navy E Award given to Perfect Circle of Hagerstown for the excellence of service during World War II, August 1944. Lothair Teetor, left and George Keagy, right, hold the banner. Courtesy of Perfect Circle

An effort was made by the federal government to encourage manufacture of peacetime goods. Veterans needed jobs and the nation could not stand another depression. Perfect Circle expanded and added factories in other places. Belden made additions to their plant. Avco, Alcoa, Johns-Mansfield, Crosley, International Harvester and other manufacturing plants in Wayne County gave jobs to hundreds throughout eastern Indiana and western Ohio.

The 1960s saw many important changes for the county. A law passed by the state legislature in 1959 forced schools to consolidate. By 1962 the fifteen separate school systems had merged into five. Children were bussed from here to there until new schools were built, mostly completed in the 1970s. This change impacted the popular basketball tourney which every school fan looked forward to. Fan loyalties had to change and the

tournament reformed. It continued until 1997 when it was decided to establish class basketball tournaments based on student enrollment.

A disastrous fire in February 1965 caused an estimated damage of a million dollars to the General Telephone Company of Indiana disrupting Richmond's telephone service for several weeks. The largest disaster to strike Wayne County happened in Richmond on a sunny Saturday, the day before Palm Sunday, April 6, 1968 at 1:47 p.m. Two explosions rocked Main Street, believed to have ignited at the Marting Arms, a sports goods store at the southeast corner of Sixth and Main Streets. Eventually both a gas leak and stored gunpowder were blamed. Calls went out to the township fire departments and others came from neighboring counties. The Wayne County Fire Fighters' Association had formed in 1961 for the purpose of improving the

Wayne County Sheriff's Mounted Patrol, a volunteer group formed in 1965. Its first call to duty was to help with the disruption in vital telephone communication caused by the General Telephone Company Fire in February 1965. Courtesy of Joe Brim

training of firemen. Their cooperation and training was to be tested by the tragedy at Richmond.

Damage from the explosion was noted over a fourteen square-block area with the worst devastation contained in the one-block area around Sixth and Main streets. There were forty-one deaths of men, women and children and over one hundred injured. At the same time of the disaster, the nations cities were torn by racial strife because of the assassination of Dr. Martin Luther King Jr. But the citizens of Richmond, Wayne County and neighboring counties met this emergency with acts of courage and heroism. Black and white hands labored together with compassionate hearts. Richmond rebuilt but the downtown was never the same. It had a totally new look which earned praise from some and disappointment from others.

By 1974–1976 Wayne County was thinking of a national celebration, the two hundredth birthday of our nation. Several towns were given recognition as Bicentennial communities. Starting with the National Historic Preservation Act of 1966, there had come a new interest in the preserving of historic buildings and districts. The Levi Coffin House is a National Historic Landmark. Two Richmond neighborhoods, Old Richmond Historic District and the Starr District have been placed on the national Register of Historic Places. Historic Hagerstown Inc. opened a musuem in 1974. The home of the Overbeck Sisters in Cambridge City has been restored and the Overbeck Museum was established in the library. Historic Centerville, Inc. cares for the old Salisbury Log Courthouse and the Mansion House. Greensfork has recently

Aerial view of downtown Richmond after an explosion on April 6, 1968. The arrows indicate where township fire departments were assigned. There were ten fire departments in the county, all who came to aid in the disaster. The *Graphic* newspaper called it "Their finest hour." Courtesy of C. A. Wills

Greensfork Bicentennial Commemorative envelope and coin honor the two hundredth anniversay of the nation 1776–1976.
Courtesy of Phyllis Beers

formed a historical society. The Wayne County Historical Museum, one of the finest museums in the state, opened in 1929.

Wayne County's Century of Progress has seen many changes. Both rural and urban residents support their community organizations. They picnic, walk, play in the many parks and sports fields built over the past century. The soul is ministered to by the establishments of several Protestant, Catholic, Mormon and Jewish congregations. Culture is offered through the Richmond Symphony Orchestra, the Richmond Art Museum, Whitewater Opera Company, lectures, theater and guest artist concerts. Higher education is available from Earlham College, the Earlham School of Religion, Bethany Seminary, Indiana University East and Ivy Technical Vocational School. Wayne County has continued to achieve as it did in its first century, providing a good quality of life for its citizens.

An Abington threshing ring using a Richmond-built Gaar-Scott threshing machine, 1920. William Smoker and his son Oscar owned and operated the machine for about twenty-five years. The Smoker family were early settlers in Abington Township. Courtesy of Melvin Smoker

Chapter 3

Abington Township

In 1805, John Cox from Kentucky purchased the land which is now the site of the village of Abington. It was laid out in 1817 and officially recorded in 1818. Abington Township was organized in 1837 and was the thirteenth township to be formed in Wayne County. There has never been a large population in Abington Township. For a short time in the early 1800s there was a village named Bethlehem located in the southwest corner of section 24, but it did not last. In 1850 Abington village reached its largest population of two hundred six. There are now about one hundred twenty residents living in town.

Abington village grew as settlers bought property and cleared the land. Business developed when items were needed which the settlers could not produce for themselves. In the days before roads were built there were only trails through the forest. It was difficult to take corn, flax and wheat for long distances to be milled. As the farms prospered, mills were built to process the grain. Prosperity of the homestead farms enabled the village to grow and by 1827 Abington had a fulling mill (for thickening and shearing home-made flannel), a carding machine for combing wool, a general store, two taverns, blacksmith and gunsmith.

Turnpikes were built and railroads came through Wayne County in the 1840s and 1850s but Abington was left behind. No good roads led to the county seat of Centerville and later Richmond, which became the hubs for shipping goods. By 1870 there were only one hundred eighty-one residents in the village. But the people of the township continued to thrive and maintain a high interest in their community. Six schools were established, eventually becoming consolidated into the last school (1–8 grades) which was

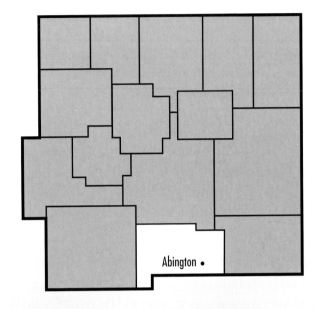

Year formed: 1837

Town: Abington, unincorporated

1990 Township Population: 865

Size: 22 square miles

Waterways: East branch of Whitewater River, Elkhorn Creek,

Topography: West and central rolling; East side hilly with a fertile valley along the Whitewater River.

Main roads: U.S. 27, Potter Shop Road, Abington Pike

A Pictorial History of Wayne County, Indiana

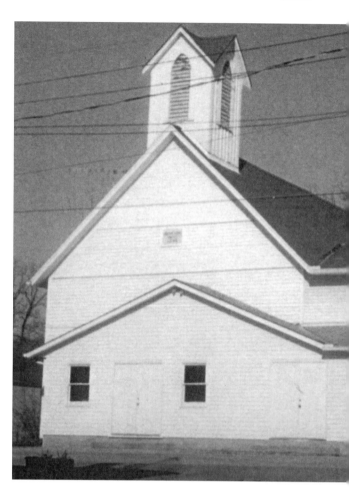

Lamb homestead, circa 1814, is one of the oldest structures in eastern Indiana. James Lamb, a Revolutionary soldier, came to Wayne County in 1811 where he built this large limestone house with walls at least two feet thick. The house stands in the northeastern part of Abington Township. Courtesy of Wayne County Museum

The Smith-Esteb House, 1917. Mr. and Mrs. David Esteb gave it to the county for a tuberculosis hospital in memory of Mr. and Mrs. George Smith, parents of Mrs. Esteb. Mrs. Esteb gave $100,000 and the sanitarium was open from 1934–1958. It became a home for aged persons until 1975. Courtesy of Wayne County Museum

The Abington Christian Church, built in 1871, stands near the Whitewater River in the town of Abington. It is the only remaining active church in Abington and is in the center of town. Courtesy of Libby Rusk

Abington Township School, built in 1922, consolidated six small schools. It is located three miles north of Abington at the corner of Smoker Road. In 1962 Abington consolidated with Centerville. The school was used until 1985. Photo by Carolyn Lafever

built in 1922. Abington and Centerville Schools consolidated in 1961. Abington held elementary classes until it was closed in 1985.

One of the most interesting and scenic drives in Wayne County is along the Abington Pike, just north of the village. In the spring there is a profusion of wild flowers, redbud trees and a wandering creek which makes one want to stop and wade in the water. Another interesting Abington Township feature was the double-span iron bridge built across the Whitewater River on the east side of the town. It was erected in 1881. The old iron bridge was replaced in 1990, which took away the steep grade of the hill and the sharp horseshoe curve as one entered Abington from the east.

The Willing Workers, a popular organization in Abington, was started in 1919 by the Christian Church. Some of them are in front of the Abington school resting from one of their many community projects. Circa 1940s. Courtesy of Marilyn Kelley

The first Abington General Store opened about 1880. The present owners are Linda and William Paddock. The torch and oval Standard sign is a familiar landmark to travelers in the area although gasoline is no longer available in Abington. Courtesy of Libby Rusk

Abington's town fountain and horse drinking trough, built in 1903, replaced an earlier wooden one. People could refresh themselves when they came to shop or to church in Abington. The fountain was recently found to be impure for drinking. The Abington Fire House is at the right. Photo by Carolyn Lafever

Abington Township has no post office today but it did until at least 1895. Residents of the township now receive their mail through the Centerville, Richmond and Brownsville post offices. Although Abington is a quiet village, it continues to have an interesting community life. The Abington Christian church, built in 1871, has an active ministry in the village and the area. From 1919 women calling themselves The Willing Workers, raised funds for the school and church. When the schools consolidated and the church became stronger financially, they disbanded in the 1970s. Although this group was organized by the church, it drew in all women of the community for fellowship and community support.

The Abington Volunteer Fire Department building was built in 1972 by raising funds from the community and without the help of tax money. It has the distinction of being the first of the Volunteer Fire Departments in Wayne County and the first in Indiana to have two female firefighters join the Volunteer Firefighters team. It wasn't easy for Shirley Corder and Judith Gilmore to achieve status as active firefighters. The twenty-two man department agreed to have them join their team. They had been thoroughly trained, non-paid reserves for the department since its organization in 1968. But the township trustee (a woman) and the advisory board refused. It took a discrimination suit in 1977 to settle the matter and Abington welcomed the first women in the state to be given this status. An active volunteer firefighter receives pay allowances and benefits.

When the new bridge was opened in 1991, Abington went all out to celebrate. County officials and a host of well-wishers gathered for the festivities. Abington had its one and only parade

The Abington Township Volunteer Fire Dept., 1997, twenty years after Shirley Corder and Judith Gilmore won the right to be come active volunteer firefighters. They were the first women in Wayne County to achieve this status. Courtesy of Linda Paddock

The old double-span iron bridge for the crossing of the Whitewater River was located east of the town of Abington on Potter Shop Road. It was built in 1881, removed in 1990 and was the longest Wayne County road bridge. Courtesy of Inezetta Stiver

Abington's new bridge opened in 1991 to replace the iron bridge which had been used for over one hundred years. Bridge construction workers stayed in Abington and became friends with many of the local people. Courtesy of Joe Toney

The town of Abington nestled in its little valley, was photographed in the spring of 1997 by Joe Toney. He took the picture while on a balloon ride over the township. Courtesy of Joe Toney

ever. Another tradition was started because of the interest in the bridge. For the month of December, Abington is transformed into a Christmas Village of Lights. Trees are decorated with lights and luminaries glowing softly on both sides of the street from the bridge to the top of the hill. Hundreds of visitors come to see the lights.

Monday through Saturday a visitor can stop in Abington to visit one of the last small general stores in the county. You can have a cup of coffee, a sandwich and buy a few staples. Paddock's Store is a meeting place where one can catch up on local affairs and sense the old-time spirit of a rural and small town community. The Fire Department sounds its whistle at noon each day, letting the people know they are ready if needed. Abington Township remains primarily a rural farm township with many attractive farms and homes.

The Boston Inn, September 27, 1931. Sunday after the tornado destroyed Boston High School on Friday. Joe Toney was in the school when the tornado struck and his father owned the Boston Inn. Business was good that day because hundreds of automobiles paraded by to see the tornado damage. Courtesy of Joe Toney

Boston Township

Boston Township lies in the extreme southeast corner of Wayne County. Some of the county's earliest settlers came here in 1806. Most settled along the Elkhorn Creek and their community became known as the "Kentucky Settlement." These, along with Rue and Holman, a few miles north, and David Hoover's group of Quakers at Richmond, were influencial in promoting the anti-slavery cause in Indiana.

The early settlers found an abundance of wild game which included buffalo, deer and elk. They settled along Elkhorn Creek because of the many natural springs and good drainage. Elkhorn Creek runs diagonally across the township with the twenty-foot high Elkhorn Falls located about midway. This waterway was named for a large set of elk horns found near the mouth of the creek. There are two prehistoric earth works or mounds in the township and many areas of woodlands including a classified forest.

The first school in Wayne County was started in 1807, located at what is now the Elkhorn Cemetery. The first church congregation in Wayne County was established there by Baptist minister, Lazarus Whitehead, in 1806. Boston Township had many firsts in Wayne County because of its southern location. Early settlers came to the newly formed county on trails from Cincinnati and southern Ohio.

There were at one time six schools in the township. By 1922 they were consolidated into one twelve-year school, the Boston Consolidated Schools, located at the town of Boston. On September 25, 1931, Friday afternoon just before the children would be dismissed from school, a tornado moved in from the west. It struck the school buildings and roofs crashed down upon several classrooms. There were more than two

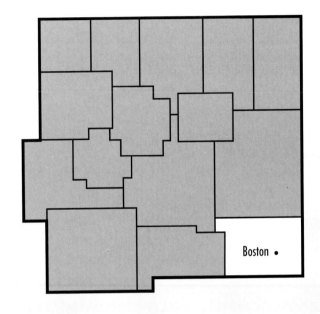

Boston •

Year formed: 1835

Town: Boston

1990 Township Population: 917

Size: 24.5 square miles

Waterways: Elkhorn Creek

Topography: North and west, rolling hills; Southeast originally swampy now desirable farm land.

Main roads: Indiana 227, 122 and U.S. 27.

A Pictorial History of Wayne County, Indiana

The Elkhorn Mill, 1850-1909, was known as the "Relief Mills," and later the Wolfe Mill. It was beside the Elkhorn Falls. Mill stones from the grist mill shown on the left are now on the lawn of the Wayne County Historical Museum. Courtesy of Wayne County Museum

Entrance to Rudolph Leeds' lodge and recreation area, circa 1910. Leeds was editor and publisher of the Palladium-Item. The stone was taken from Elkhorn Creek and it was built like early stone fences. Fence builders of the 1830s named Fromm built many of the stone fences in Boston and Abington townships. Courtesy of Carolyn Lafever

Elkhorn Falls and a stone bridge in the 1890's. The falls, located near Indiana 227 were 20-25 feet high. A blacksmith shop is beside the falls. Courtesy of Marilyn Kelley

Elkhorn Baptist Church, built about 1900, was on the site of the first church in Wayne County, 1805. The first school house was built near by. Many early settlers are buried in the Elkhorn Cemetery where the church once stood. The church closed in 1936 and was removed in 1961. Photograph by Carolyn Lafever

hundred students in the two buildings, but fortunately only a few were injured enough to be hospitalized. The grade school building was repaired but the high school had to be replaced. Several other buildings were damaged and the little town of Boston became a focus of concern for the whole county.

For many years the Boston School was a center of community activities, sports and fund raisers. When the new school districts in Wayne County were formed, Boston School became part of the Richmond Community Schools. Boston was used as a middle school until it was closed in 1962. The remaining school in the township is the Garrison Elementary School, kindergarten through fifth, on Niewoehner Road.

The town of Boston, platted in 1832, was first called Salem, then New Boston and by the turn of the century, just Boston. There are three churches in Boston, the United Methodist built in 1868, the Christian Church established in 1881 and the most recent, the Old Time Holiness Church. A post office was established in 1837 and is still active. Boston was on the main road from Richmond to Cincinnati and for several years a stage line operated through it. The oldest house in town was built in 1808 and was later used as a stage coach depot and inn for overnight travelers. In 1865 the road through Boston was a toll road and the house stood at the main intersection where the toll was collected.

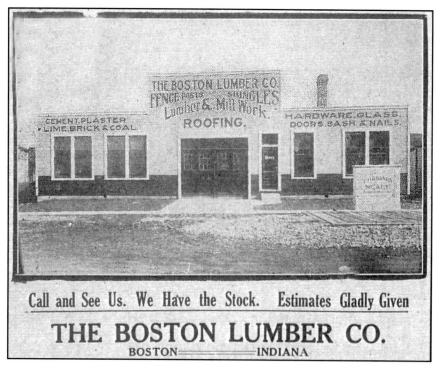

The Boston Lumber Co., advertisement from the Clevenger's Directory of Farmers and Breeders of Wayne County 1919. Courtesy of Ethel Sieweke

Boston High School, right, before the tornado struck on Sept. 25, 1931. Note the section with the curved top decoration, which was a direct hit by the tornado. Courtesy of Joe and Verna Toney, students at the time

A rear view of the high school building after the tornado in 1931. Ninety children were injured but no fatalities. Courtesy of Verna and Joe Toney

On June 26, 1849, the dreaded disease of cholera stuck the town of one hundred twenty residents. The epidemic had been carried to Boston by stage coach passengers coming from Cincinnati. By August 3, fifty-three people had died, including whole families and five doctors who had attended them. Passenger service was stopped and the town was abandoned, but people returned when the epidemic was over.

Early business in Boston included a gunsmith, shoemaker, tailor, blacksmith, wagon maker and several doctors. Over the years other places of business have included mills, a tile factory, general stores, several dry goods stores, a bank, pool hall, ice cream parlor and barber shops. Businesses today are the Central Furniture and Carpet, Tanner's Wholesale Leather Co., C & O Auction, White's Used Auto Sales, AGP Grain Co. and a branch of the Union County Co-op. The Boston Volunteer Fire Department was established in the mid-1950s. It has three trucks housed in a building with an annex which is also used as a community building.

In 1900 the railroad came through Boston bringing employment and a new growth in population. The fifty-room Yellow Dog Hotel was

Richmond Municipal Airport, dedicated July 4, 1945 and at one time was served by three commercial airlines. A sky diving school has headquarters there. Courtesy of the Richmond Municipal Airport

Boston Christian Church Pastor, Don Brammer, hugs Judith Vilhauer, 52, in this 1995 photo. The crutches were for a sprained ankle. Mrs. Vilhauer, an instructor at Indiana University East and Ivy Tech, had just completed her Doctors degree in mathematics. The church honored her for this accomplishment. She died unexpectedly in early 1996. Courtesy of Marilyn Kelley

Bill Magaw, seated, and Russian artist Andrei Volkov in 1986, working on a metal sculpture at Magaw's studio in Boston. Bill Magaw is internationally known for his wood and metal sculpture. Courtesy of Bill and Jeanne Magaw

built for the families of the railroad builders. Others lived in abandoned box cars. In 1927 the National Telephone and Telegraph Co. built a "lead line" through the entire length of the township. The line runs from Kansas City to Pittsburgh.

Another addition to the Boston Township was the Richmond Municipal Airport built in 1945. Military planes used the airfields for training flights. TWA made regular stops in 1947 and later Delta Airlines took over. In 1950 Lake Central Airlines had regular flights to Chicago. At the present time it is used only by corporation and private owners of airplanes plus a sky diving school with headquarters there.

Boston Township's resident artists are William and Jeanne Magaw, whose studio is just outside of Boston. William produces outstanding sculptures in metal and wood and has achieved international attention and awards. He and his wife, also an artist, have traveled to Mexico and Russia. They have entertained and sponsored several Russian artists who have visited and worked with them at their home in Boston.

While primarily rural in setting, Boston Township has many fine homes built and owned by people who work in Richmond and nearby communities. There are many beautiful and productive family farms.

The Paul and Rosie Wuertemberger farm located on Indiana 227, north of Boston. The family has owned the farm of 479 acres since 1937. One of Boston Townships many prosperous farms, their primary business today is a dairy herd of 145 cows. Photo by Ed Lafever

Centerville, May 1900. Decoration Day parade, moving west at the corner of Morton and Main. The old Courthouse is on the left. The band is followed by veterans of the Mexican War, Civil War and Spanish American War. GAR families and descendants of Revolutionary War soldiers bring up the rear.
Courtesy of Inezetta Stiver

Chapter 4

Center Township

Center Township was formed by the county commissioners in 1817. The county seat was moved to the town of Centerville from Salisbury in 1818 after considerable controversy. An act passed by the new Indiana state legislature in 1816 officially designated Centerville as the seat of justice for the county of Wayne. When the county seat moved to Centerville it did not quiet the controversy and it was a few years before the town was fully accepted in this role.

During the strife surrounding the location of the county seat, Centerville developed slowly. When the county seat was finally established, the town quickly grew in size and wealth. Business found it a desirable location, physicians, lawyers and other professional men established themselves there. Centerville and the surrounding area became an eminent political center for Wayne County and the state of Indiana. By 1820 it had become a village of considerable size for its day.

For many years the earlier spelling of the town's name was *Centreville*. The spelling eventually changed to Centerville and the township to Center. Centerville was platted in 1814, making it the second oldest town in Wayne County, after Salisbury platted in 1812. Improvements came quickly to Centerville in the 1830s and 1840s. The National Road running from Washington, D.C. to St. Louis was built through Indiana in 1835–1837. Centerville was the first town in Indiana to have paved streets. In 1837 the cobblestone street, part of the National Road, was supplied by the government as a mark of distinction to the promising Wayne County capital and the thriving new town.

Centerville was originally laid out with streets one hundred feet wide with sites for the Courthouse and jail, a city hall and market place.

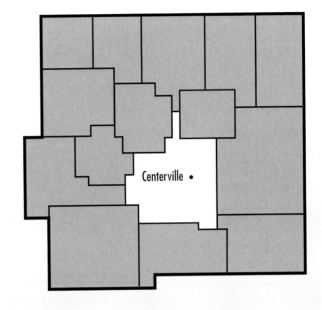

Centerville •

Year formed: 1817

Town: Centerville

1990 Township Population: 7,345

Size: 43 square miles

Waterways: Noland's Fork,

Topography: Somewhat rolling, the soil rich and productive.

Main roads: U.S. 40 and Interstate 70

A Pictorial History of Wayne County, Indiana

The fourth Wayne County courthouse stood on the corner of Main Street and Morton Avenue. The first Centerville Courthouse was of logs, this second of brick. When the county seat moved to Richmond, the building was sold and became an organ factory. It was partially destroyed by fire in 1914. Photo by C. Lafever

The old Mansion House, circa 1840s, was a popular inn along the National Road for many years. Owned by Historic Centerville Inc., it hosts an annual quilt show in June. The old Salisbury log courthouse has been moved beside the Mansion House and is being restored. Courtesy of Inezetta Stiver

Indiana's Civil War Governor, Oliver P. Morton, was born in Salisbury, but lived much of his life in Centerville. His Centerville residence, which he purchased in 1857, still stands on West Main Street and is a private residence. Courtesy of Inezetta Stiver

Centerville Depot and Elevator, circa 1900. Farmers went together to order a car load of fence. They are unloading it from a freight car. The tracks on the north side of the depot were for loading and switching. The main line ran between the depot and the elevator. Courtesy of Inezetta Stiver

In the 1890s, farm organizations were expanding. The Farmers' Institute was held in December, 1894 as a convention to share the many facets of farming. Note the earlier spelling of Centreville is used in the advertisement. Courtesy of Inezetta Stiver

The streets were soon narrowed to allow for more real estate. Building lots sold rapidly with high prices. Stagecoach and postal routes passed through on the National Road and business flourished. In the 1820s and 1830s Center Township was still being settled and the land was covered with thick forests. Indians had been a threat before Indiana became a state, but by the time the county seat was fully operating, there was little trouble with them.

Many outstanding political figures lived and worked in Centerville. They include brothers Jacob B. Julian, attorney, George W. Julian, lawyer and member of the United States Congress 1852–1871, and Isaac H. Julian, newspaper publisher in Centerville and Richmond. Oliver P. Morton, Indiana's Civil War Governor and U.S.

Senator and his Indiana Secretary of State, Judge William A. Peele, both lived and worked in Centerville. Lieutenant Commander James M. Prichett was born in Centerville in 1836. He was appointed at age sixteen to the Naval Academy at Annapolis, graduating in 1857. He served in the navy during and after the Civil War and was highly esteemed for his service record. He died in 1871. During the second world war a U.S. destroyer was named for him, the USS Prichett DD-561.

Center Township was the location for the popular Old Settlers' Picnic. One of the first Old Settler's Picnic was held in 1859 in the grove of Oliver T. Jones, a mile north of Centerville. The annual meetings continued until at least 1924 and were held at various locations around Centerville.

The L. D. Commons Stock Farm. Their advertisements stated they were "prosperous raisers of Quality horses." The famous horse, Single G, a world famous pacer was foaled here and was sold to W. B. Barefoot of Cambridge City who brought him to racing fame. Courtesy of Inezetta Stiver

The Wayne County Corn Show or Corn School of 1910, held in the town hall. The hall was used for a skating rink and for basketball games. Gas lights are enclosed with protective wire fence. Each exhibitor showed ten ears of corn and prizes were awarded for the best. Courtesy of Inezetta Stiver

Bertsch Bros. Manufacturers of Hardwood Lumber. They were dealers in wood products, iron pumps and pipe fittings. Some of the large logs available at the time are shown at the left. Courtesy of Inezetta Stiver

Wood E. Eliason's Pearl-Wood Stock Farm, 1918. Most farms did not have electricity. However about 1905 acetylene light plants were made for home use. Delco-Light and others later made battery operated power plants for farms and suburban homes. This picture was in the October 1918 issue of the Delco-Light Visitor. Courtesy of Inezetta Stiver

In 1867 a thirty-acre fairground was laid out for the Wayne County Agricultural Society. The grounds fell into decline and fairs were held in other places around the county. In 1928 a new county fairground was built south of Centerville near the old fair site. The Wayne County 4-H Fair was held there until 1975 when a tornado destroyed the buildings. The county fair was moved to its new location on north Salisbury Road, Wayne Township.

Centerville prospered until Richmond successfully laid claim to the county seat and it was moved in 1873. The county seat was originally relocated to Centerville because it was nearer the center of the county and travel to it was easier. But Richmond outstripped it in growth and tax revenue and wanted to be the county seat. All objections for again moving the county seat were put down and Richmond won the battle. From that time Centerville began to lose many of its business places and professional offices to Richmond.

Although Centerville declined when the county seat moved, the town continued to make improvements. Railroads came through in the 1850s. In 1902 a line for electric street cars was built from Richmond with a turn around at Main and Main Cross Streets (Morton Avenue). In 1903 the first interurban passed through Centerville on the route from Richmond to Indianapolis. Electric lights came to town in the winter of 1913–1914. The township had many prosperous farms, including horse farms. The world famous racing horse, Single G, was foaled on the Commons' stock farm in 1910 and sold as a two-year old to W. B. Barefoot of Cambridge City.

A Pictorial History of Wayne County, Indiana

Postcards were sent as Christmas greetings from the Psi Iota Xi Sorority in 1944 to the local young people in the armed forces of World War II. Collection of Carolyn Lafever

In 1964 Centerville commemorated one hundred fifty years with a large celebration. On a Sunday the congregation of the Centerville Christian Church dressed in costume to celebrate the occasion. They are posed in front of the church which faces Morton Avenue. Courtesy of Inezetta Stiver

Buildings of the Wayne County Fairgrounds at the south edge of Centerville near the school grounds. The annual county fair was held here from 1929–1975 when a tornado demolished the buildings. The fair grounds were moved to the present site on Salisbury Road in Wayne Township. Courtesy of Centerville Library

In 1920 Claude Berry, who had built the first airport near Richmond, purchased a tract of land southeast of Centerville. Hangers were built and gas pumps installed. Runways were graded and several planes were housed there. Shortly after it opened the airport was used as a test field for planes built by the Davis Aircraft Corporation, a Richmond industry located at Seventh and Richmond Avenue. In 1930 the factory closed when a fire destroyed several planes and the federal government installed a weather station at the airfield.

In 1932, John Nixon, who purchased the airport property from Berry, and Wilfred Jessup, owner of the abandoned fairgrounds next to the airport, combined the properties into the Nixon Airport. There was agitation to have the city of Richmond purchase the airport and arrangements

were made to purchase it. In 1942 during World War II, the Civil Air Patrol designated Richmond as a group Headquarters. But the C.A.P. determined that the Centerville Airport would not be suitable and it was closed. Another location in Boston Township was selected for Richmond's Municipal Airport.

An important event for all the people of Center Township was the consolidation of the Wayne County schools in 1959–1962. Each township in the county had a school and twelve townships had high schools. With the new consolidation there would be only five school corporations. Abington and Center formed the Centerville-Abington School Corporation with the schools now located at Centerville. Rose Hamilton Elementary is on Round Barn Road. New buildings have been built in Centerville and

A Pictorial History of Wayne County, Indiana

The Eliason Homestead, purchased 1814 by Joshua Eliason. The barn was built in 1844, the brick house in 1896. The farm, located three miles north east of Centerville, has passed to the youngest son for four generations. Today it is farmed by Donald D. Eliason and son Douglas Eliason, 4th & 5th generation. Courtesy of Inezetta Stiver

Centerville-Abington School Corporation, 1995. All the schools are located here except Rose Hamilton Elementary. The old high school at the left rear of the picture is still used. Photo by Bill Wallace

an unusual round building holds the auditorium and some classrooms. The Whitewater Opera Company performed there for several years.

Many newspapers have been founded in Centerville. Some moved to other places, some changed names and others stopped because of financial reasons. The first of about twenty-two papers started in 1824 with the *Western Emporium*. The current paper, *The Centerville Crusader*, started in 1967. Joel and Carrol Rhodes owned it for several years and the current editor is Annie Glenn.

Centerville is one of the oldest towns in Wayne County and in 1971 the Centerville Historic District was accepted in the National Register of Historic Places. Historic Centerville, Inc. acquired the 1840s Mansion House Inn in 1975. The Mansion House was for many years an inn along the National Road. The latest project of Historic Centerville is to restore the old Salisbury log Courthouse on the grounds of the Mansion

House. Centerville, with its charming archways and old buildings, is considered as one of the best places for antiques shopping. Webb's Antique Mall is one of the largest in the country.

About one third of Center Township's residents live in Centerville. There are several housing additions being built in the township. Although not within the corporation, these "fringe areas" contain almost as many residents as the town. Centerville is adding an interceptor sewer line to meet the needs of this growing community.

Greens Fork depot, stockyards and elevator, circa 1920s. Courtesy of Malcolm Jeffers

Chapter 5

Clay Township

Ask people around Clay Township where their first job was and many will say it was detasseling corn on one of the hybrid seed corn farms. Clay Township was one of the first in Indiana to produce hybrid seed corn on a large scale. The knowledge of improving corn by crossing two varieties to make a hybrid was discovered before 1920, but not put into practical use until the early 1930s. In 1935, farmer Ted Davis and Wayne County Agricultural Agent Scott Milligan obtained approval from Purdue University for ten high school students from Economy and Greens Fork to grow one acre apiece of hybrid seed corn. The Greens Fork students were Porter Davis, Josephine Davis, Albert Hunnicutt, Richard Cranor and Gale Gilmer. The Economy students were Ed Cain, John Cloud, Charles Powell, Ray Mendenhall and Gene Franklin.

The experiment to produce hybrid seed corn was successful. The students helped plant, detassel and harvested the seed. From this first trial came several successful hybrid seed corn farms. Albert Hunnicutt, Richard Cranor and Porter Davis owned farms in Clay Township. Eugene Barrett of Hagerstown, Everett Hunt and Frank Hodgin of the Whitewater area and Ralph Rank of southern Wayne County were also in the seed corn business.

Through the years, for about two weeks in early summer, hands were needed to detassel the corn so that it would pollinate properly. Many teens found work on the seed corn farms, a hard two weeks but the pay was good. All the growers in Wayne County except Davis Seed Farms had quit the business by 1985.

Clay was one of the later townships, formed in 1831, but settlers had come as early as 1809. In 1818 Thomas Hatfield platted the town of Washington, choosing one of the most honored

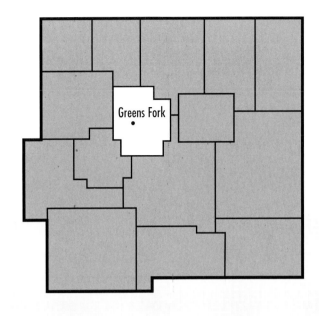

Year formed: 1831

Town: Greens Fork

1990 Township Population: 1,042

Size: 20 square miles

Waterways: Greens Fork, Morgan Creek

Topography: Some flat area, hilly and rolling along the waterways.

Main roads: U.S. 38

A Pictorial History of Wayne County, Indiana

Huge logs being brought to sawmills near Greens Fork about 1900. A rare sight to see one log fill the complete wagon. Courtesy of Malcolm Jeffers

Etta Dean Millinery Shop, south side of Pearl Street, next door to her husband's store, T. A. Dean jeweler. Circa 1910. Today the building is Carolyn's Restaurant. Courtesy of Porter Davis

Pearl Street (Indiana 38) at Main and Pearl facing east, 1903. Several buildings on the left were destroyed by fire in 1912. Courtesy of Malcolm Jeffers

and familiar names on the frontier. The waterway running on the west side of town was called Greens Fork Creek after a notorious Indian who took the name of John Green. He has been described as living in a cave near Greens Fork, accused of murdering a man, running a tavern at Economy and various other exploits. But for some reason, out of respect or fear, Green's name became attached to important parts of Clay Township.

In 1889 Washington's name was changed to Green's Fork to prevent post office confusion with another Washington, Indiana. Later the town board dropped the apostrophe in the word Greens. But there was still confusion. Sometimes the name would be spelled as one word, as two words with an apostrophe or as it should be. Even the road department couldn't get it right. After repeated prompting almost everyone spells it correctly.

Greens Fork was a prosperous town in 1912, according to an article written by S. D. Neff. There were three grocery stores, two meat markets, a blacksmith shop, hardware store, three halls and one opera house. Three hotels were open, two restaurants, a five-and-ten cent store and the list goes on. The town had telephones but no electricity. One could come to Greens Fork for just about anything needed including medical care. The year before in 1911 Greens Fork hosted its first fall festival which brought a crowd of about four thousand people.

The First World War and the depression of the 1930s caused drastic changes for everyone. Greens Fork was no exception. The development of the seed farms in Clay Township in the later years of the depression brought encouragement to the area.

Even the post office had a hard time deciding how to spell Greens Fork. It was finally decided to spell the town's name
GREENS FORK. Courtesy of Porter Davis

Greens Fork School built in 1908. Greens Fork is credited with making one of the first township consolidations in Indiana in
1888. Collection of Carolyn Lafever

Hotel and restaurant next to the Drug Store in Greens Fork, circa 1910. A town pump is in front with a bucket for horses to drink. A tin cup hanging behind the man is for thirsty humans. The buildings burned in the fire of 1912. Courtesy of Malcolm Jeffers

Greens Fork's first schoolhouse in 1877 was considered one of the most modern in the state. They were first to transport children in a hack provided by the school in 1885. In 1908 a new school building was opened and in 1910 it was commissioned as a high school called the Greens Fork High School. Additions were made to the building in 1924–1925. The sports teams were called the Greens Fork Demons. One local wag declared they had to have a tough-sounding name to battle such foes as the Richmond Red Devils and the Hagerstown Tigers. The community was particularly proud of its basketball team of 1936. The scrappy team from a small high school defeated Richmond at the Sectional Tournament. They went on to whip the Muncie Bearcats at the Regional but were taken down by New Castle. Nineteen thirty-six is still remembered as a special year for Greens Fork High School.

From 1959–1963 the Wayne County School Reorganization Committee had the difficult task of helping consolidate fifteen townships into five school districts. Esther Bond, secretary for the group, describes it as a sad and controversial time

Fire ripped through several buildings on Pearl Street in 1912. Greens Fork had a second fire in October. Both fires were believed to be arson. Courtesy of Malcolm Jeffers

A Pictorial History of Wayne County, Indiana

Greens Fork Lumber Company, circa 1930. It was destroyed by fire. Courtesy of Malcolm Jeffers

Allen and Cain Blacksmithing in Greens Fork, circa 1912. Automobiles became more common and blacksmiths had to become more varied in their services. Courtesy of Malcolm Jeffers

D. W. Harris Produce and Feed, 1919. Greens Fork was well known as a poultry center for feed and a hatchery. Posed by the cars on the left is Dan W. Harris, owner. This business was located on the east side of the elevator. Courtesy of Malcolm Jeffers

GOOD INDIANA HYBRIDS PAY

Out State Hybrids Usually Not Adapted to Indiana Soil
and Climatic Conditions

BOOST YOUR CORN PROFITS
With Indiana Hybrid Seed

Highest Quality
Thoroughly Dried

Certified by Indiana Corn Growers Association

Carefully Graded
Properly Made

Growing Indiana Certified Hybrids Adapted
to Your Locality Means:

More Bushels per Acre.

Stiffer Stalks to Reduce Lodging.

More Extensive and Stronger Root Systems.

Elimination of Barren Stalks.

Resistance to Drouth and Extreme Temperatures.

Greater Foliage with Smaller Stalks Increases Yields.

Increased Disease Resistance.

Increased Insect Resistance.

Improved Quality of Grain.

Ears Borne at Uniform Height, Making Husking Easier.

T. C. DAVIS

GREENS FORK, — INDIANA

2½ Miles Southwest   Phone Greens Fork

MEMBER OF

Indiana Hybrid Growers Association, Inc.
and
Ind. Co-Operative Hybrid Producers, Inc.

CHECKING THE COUNTY CORN TEST PLOT

Tests of this kind throughout the State, conducted by the Agricultural Extension Department in co-operation with County Agents and farmers, have proved conclusively that INDIANA CERTIFIED HYBRIDS out-yield all open-pollenated varieties of Corn as well as competitive Hybrids. Your County Agricultural Agent can give you valuable information as to the best adapted Hybrids to use in your community.

Davis Seed Corn advertisement, 1938. Courtesy of Porter Davis

because several communities would lose their schools. The sound of children at school would not be heard in Greens Fork after 1971 when it was closed. The children attend the Nettle Creek Schools in Hagerstown.

Recovering from the loss of their school has been difficult for many communities. Greens Fork lost its last grocery store in the 1980s. But some of the business community has remained strong. Tom Bond operates Bond's Wool, Fur and Root which buys fur pelts, wool and wild roots. There used to be many people who hunted and trapped as an added income. Most hunters and trappers today do it as a sport. Bond is one of only

a few fur buyers left in the state and most of the fur comes from raccoons. With a resurgence of deer population in the 1970–1980s, deer hides are being sold. Coyotes, while not quality fur animals, have followed the deer into Wayne County and their night barking is often reported in the rural areas. The Bonds were early settlers in Clay Township. Tom Bond Jr. lives on the farm on Mineral Springs Road homesteaded by his ancestor Jesse Bond in 1813.

The local churches have played an important part in Clay Township's history. Many years ago there was a little community northwest of Greens Fork known as Sugar Grove. A school was located

A Pictorial History of Wayne County, Indiana

Sugar Grove Church. The site once had two churches side by side, split by a denomination dispute in 1889. A fire in 1942 took one and then the congregations merged to become the Sugar Grove Community Church. Photo by Ed Lafever

Marta Davis proudly displays a large ear of hybrid seed corn raised by her father, Porter Davis, 1955. Courtesy of Porter Davis

Greens Fork Community Center, built in 1985. The building was a gift to the people of Clay Township from Glenn and Blanche Veal. The old Greens Fork School Bell has a place of honor in front of the Center. Photo by Ed Lafever

there and for a time there were two churches side by side with the same name, Sugar Grove United Brethren. At first there was only one church, but in 1889 the domination split in part on the issue of membership in secret societies. A bitter feud erupted at Sugar Grove between the Radicals and the Liberals. Finally a court decision was made in favor of the Liberals who owned the church and all the property.

Not to be outdone, a farmer donated land on the south side of the church. The Radicals built a church on the property. Members of each attended their church and declared that the other group "was not to be trusted." The stalemate continued until 1942 when fate took a hand. The Radical church burned down. Finally there came a resolution to the feud and after a long negotiation with both denominations, the two congregations came together. However they were no longer United Brethren, a poor description of their past association, but the non-denominational Sugar Grove Community Church.

There are at least four active churches in Clay Township. A product of one local church, Blanche Kerr Brock was born in Greens Fork and her husband, Virgil, served a pastor for the Greens Fork Christian church while he attended Earlham College in Richmond. They combined their talents in ministry for fifty years and composed many Gospel songs, the most famous being, "Beyond The Sunset."

Greens Fork celebrated the national Bicentennial in 1976 with a four-day event. Ted Davis, the Grand Marshal, rode with Dr. William E. Upchurch in his 1929 Ford convertible. Chauncy Cranor rode in the rumble seat. Dr. Upchurch, well known in Wayne County for the Greens Fork Veterinary Hospital, passed away

unexpectedly in 1997. He helped sponsor a pet cemetery which was opened in 1982 at the edge of Greens Fork.

The town of Greens Fork has been aggressive in trying to revitalize itself. New business places have opened and several of the old buildings have been refurbished. The Community Center sponsors activities throughout the year. Three issues of a local newspaper called the *Claytonian*, have been issued since 1976 which contain interesting historical information. A historical society was recently organized to preserve the interesting heritage of this community.

Dr. William Upchurch, veterinarian, and Jerry Adams examines one of Adams' pigs. Dr. Upchurch's office and home are at the east edge of Greens Fork. Upchurch passed away in 1997. Hagerstown Exponent photo

Dalton School reunion, circa 1926. The Dalton School was closed in 1968 and has been converted into a private residence. Courtesy of Jane Peirce Lesh

Chapter 6

Dalton Township

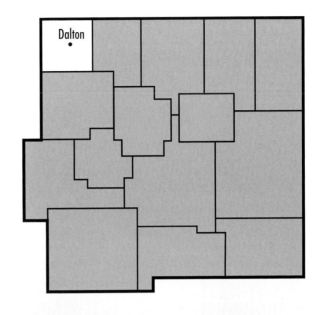

alton Township was formed from Perry in 1847 and is in the northwest corner of Wayne County. It is the next to the smallest township, Webster being smallest. Most of the land within Dalton was not for sale to settlers until 1822 since only a small strip on the east side was part of the Twelve Mile Purchase in 1809. Settlers had come to the area as early as 1818. Aquila West was the first and his farm was near the town of the present Dalton. Some of the early settlers had to leave their claims when the land was sold by the Government because they could not pay the price.

Most of Dalton Township is a wide ridge of hills separating two valleys. Nettle Creek is on the west and part of the west branch of the Whitewater River, also known as West River, is on the east. Many Indian artifacts have been found along sections of West River, leading some to believe there were Indian settlements or summer camp sites there. The valleys are fertile and have some excellent farm land. The West River valley is narrow and steep hills rises on both sides and the creek is prone to flooding.

Dalton was platted in 1828 by Joseph Davis and Tense Massey. Other additions were made later. The first store in Dalton was started by Aaron Mills and the first in Franklin was set up by Benjamin F. Beeson. The initial post office in 1832 was in Franklin and called Palymyra. It was moved to Dalton after much argument and named the Dalton Post Office. In 1876 Franklin obtained its own post office which lasted a few years. Dalton's post office closed in the early 1900s .

Several mills were built in Dalton Township between 1824 to 1853. The best known mill site is on the Jefferson-Dalton township line. It was built by Daniel Ulrich as a grist mill. He replaced it with machinery for a woolen factory and in 1854 sold

Year formed: 1847

Town: Dalton, Unincorported

1990 Township Population: 580

Size: 16 square miles

Waterways: West River, Nettle Creek

Topography: Ridge of hills separating two valleys

Main roads: US 35, Indiana 1

A Pictorial History of Wayne County, Indiana

Butchering day in Dalton Township, circa 1898. Neighbors worked together on this hard job. Butchering was done in cold weather to preserve the meat. It was then smoked, canned or salted for use over the next few months. Courtesy of Jane Peirce Lesh

Benjamin Beeson (1843–1902) a son of Isaac and Mary Beeson. He helped form the Dalton and Hagerstown Turnpike. In the 1890s, he published a Prohibitionist paper in Richmond called *The Richmond Enterprise.* His paper supported the Temperance movement against alcohol. Courtesy of Mildred Thornburg

Nettle Creek Friends Church, circa 1900. The church traditionally had two doors, one for men, one for women. There were two sections inside for them to sit separately. The room was eventually altered so that all can now sit where they choose. Courtesy of Thelma and Kenny Smith

The Losantville band, circa 1889, poses with John Baldwin's partially inflated balloon at the Dalton Fair. The Spanish American War veteran gave balloon shows during the fair season. Baldwin was killed in 1905 at the Greenville, Ohio Fair. Collection of Carolyn Lafever

it to William and Josiah Test. It was a successful business manufacturing jeans, satinets, cassimeres, flannels, blankets and yarn. The mill property was sold to Benjamin Parsons in 1899. He turned it into a profitable meat slaughtering business which continued in the family for many years.

Although Dalton and Franklin filed plat papers, neither had more than seventy-five residents. For a time Dalton had several small businesses and the Dalton Steam-Mill Company's mill was located near by. For a time Franklin grew faster than Dalton. Several Beeson brothers set up businesses there in the 1820–1830s and it was known as "Beeson Town." Between 1830 and 1870 there were four doctors in Franklin and eight in Dalton making the township an early medical center for the area.

Business flourished in Franklin and Dalton until about 1840 when the bottom fell out of pork prices. The pioneers produced too many products and speculation was high. But the markets were far away and transportation was expensive. Overproduction wrecked the business and facto-

Bert Wilkinson, owner of the Dalton General Store, 1959. He was always prepared to make a hot dog sandwich for a child who didn't want to eat at the school cafeteria. His store was destroyed by fire and not rebuilt. Collection of Carolyn Lafever

Farm home of Suzanne and Webster Craig was built for George Thornburg in 1904. Located near Thornburg Station, a flag stop on the C & O. railroad. The farm was homesteaded by the Thornburgs in 1827 and owned by the family until 1936. Courtesy of Suzanne and Webster Craig

Tom Thumb Wedding given by the children at Dalton, 1944. It was performed in the summer for a Farm Bureau meeting. Elementary schools performed Tom Thumb weddings as early as the 1920s. The children performed a genuine little wedding with all the trimmings. Courtesy of Flossie Lafever

West River Friends Meeting and cemetery, 1960. Organized in 1825, the building was built in 1882. The flower garden in the shape of a cross was laid out by Ralph Waltz in 1960 and is still maintained. Courtesy of Irene Black

ries of the Beeson brothers. Business sharply declined in the villages and Franklin did not recover. Dalton stayed a bit more prosperous but both now are only crossroads with a few houses.

From 1880–1891 the Dalton Fair was sponsored by the Wayne, Henry & Randolph County Agricultural Association. It boasted exhibits and competitions but would not allow horse racing. The Dalton Fair had a large attendance for several years. One of the attractions at the fair of 1889 was a balloon demonstration by aeronaut Prof. Johnny Baldwin. He was a Dalton boy who served in the Balloon Corp. during the Spanish American War. It was reported that he made the signals from his balloon when Theodore Roosevelt made his famous charge up San Juan hill in Cuba. Baldwin was a local hero and celebrity.

In 1905 Baldwin performed at fairs all over the country. His final appearance was on September 1 at the Greenville, Ohio fair making his 1,201 balloon ascension. Part of the performance was to throw out lighted dynamite sticks to show how the military could bomb targets from above. The balloon had barely reached the proper height when something went very wrong. All the dynamite sticks blew up, balloon and Baldwin with them. The tragedy stunned the fair crowd and his home community. His wife never recovered from the shock and died shortly after. Their three young daughters, who had seen the explosion, were sent the Knightstown Children's Home. The Dalton Fair closed in 1891, losing out to the Wayne County Fair at Hagerstown, where a fine horse racing track had been built.

A Pictorial History of Wayne County, Indiana

Robert and Elsie Peirce. Robert was honored as a Sagamore of the Wabash in 1986 for his work with the Indiana Covered Bridge Society. He is well known as a genealogist. Elsie Davis Peirce was a descendant of Joseph Davis, one of Dalton's first settlers. Courtesy of Robert Peirce

The Kopper Kettle, a quarter mile east of St. Rd. 1 on St. Rd. 35 was owned from 1948–1972 by Fred and Martha Johnson. It was widely known for the Kopper Kettle Steak and butterscotch pie. There have been several owners since 1972. Courtesy of Joyce Johnson Farmer

The Beeson Sisters, Marjorie Conway, Mildred Thornburg, and Mary Alice Gilmer began their singing trio in the 1920s and are shown in front of the Dalton School in 1995. Well known throughout the state in their younger years, they continued to sing together until the Marjorie's death in 1996. Courtesy of Mildred Thornburg

Several churches were established in Dalton Township. Two were built by Quakers, the West River Friends Meeting, 1825, and the Nettle Creek Friends Meeting, 1828. Both congregations are still active. A United Brethren, Methodist and Baptist churches were active for a time. The first school was established by the Friends. By 1900 there were four township schools. In 1911 a new school building was built in Dalton combining three and leaving West River as the last one room school. In 1926 an addition was made to Dalton and West River was closed. Dalton school had eight grades and high school students went to Hagerstown. Dalton Township became part of the Nettle Creek School Corporation in 1962. The school closed in 1968 and the children attend classes at Hagerstown.

The North Street of Bethel, 1909. One gas light and a couple of business buildings are shown. Photo by Ed Lafever

Franklin Township

Franklin Township is in the northeastern corner of Wayne County. It was formed in 1834 from a portion of New Garden Township. The first settler, Isaac Commons from North Carolina and member of the Friends Society, is believed to have come as early as 1808–1809 settling a few miles south of Whitewater. The area grew slowly until about 1815 after the Indian wars were over. Although early Wayne County was covered with dense forest, pioneers coming to settle near Whitewater found a few buffalo and a "buffalo wallow" at Cart Road between Whitewater Road and Wallace Road. Many buffalo bones have been found at this watering or wallowing place.

In 1817 James Harlan and sons established the Harlan settlement. It was renamed Bethel in 1844 after the nearby Bethel church. Bethel was formally laid out and platted in 1850. The village was never large but had general stores and other small businesses. At one time a tile factory was located in the western part of Bethel. The last grocery store went out of business in 1969. The Post Office began in 1848 but was phased out by 1900. *The Bethel Times* newspaper owned and published by L. T. Constable and was being printed in 1942. It was printed for a few months.

The Bethel Christian Church, organized 1821, is one of the earliest Christian congregations (denomination) in the state and a historical marker describes it as the oldest of its kind north of U.S. 40. The present building was built in 1894. An event which drew many people to Bethel was the annual homecoming and old fashioned singing day at the Bethel Christian Church. It began about 1855 with a "singing class," a popular activity in many churches and schools. The traveling singing teacher made most

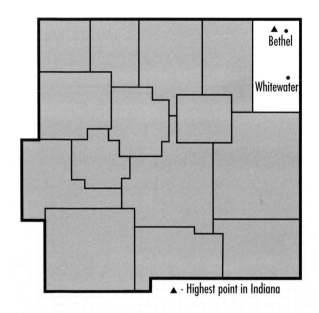

▲ - Highest point in Indiana

Year formed: 1834

Town: Whitewater; Bethel, both unincorporated

1990 Township Population: 1,306

Size: 28 Square Miles

Waterways: Middlefork of Whitewater River, West Fork of Whitewater River

Topography: Rolling hills, fertile plains

Main roads: Indiana 227; Arba Pike

A Pictorial History of Wayne County, Indiana

Bethel Christian Church, located on St. Rd. 227, organized in 1821, the first church was a log structure. A historical marker describes it as the state's oldest Christian congregation north of U.S. 40. Photo by C. Lafever

Whitewater School, circa 1960. The school was built in 1922–1923 and was both an elementary and high school. In 1954, a new addition was added to the grade school. A consolidation of Webster, New Garden, Franklin and Green was made in 1962, and is called Northeastern Wayne School Corporation. Drawing by Jack Phelps

Second church building of the Whitewater Christian Church, built in 1906–1907. The first church building burned in 1906. Photo by Carolyn Lafever

The Whitewater United Methodist Church, originally known as the First Methodist Episcopal Church. It is the oldest Methodist Church in the Richmond District, dating back to 1825. Photo by Carolyn Lafever

of his salary by selling music books to the students. At the end of the week of study, a concert was given to show what the singers had learned. Singing schools were popular from the early 1800s to as late as the 1930s. Local poet Olive Brown, author of the book, *Bloom in the Fence Row*, wrote a poem honoring the origins of Bethel's Old Fashioned Singing reunion. The poem sums up the activities of the day:

....So on this annual day in June
With basket dinner served at noon
Good friends come back each year to meet
And linger in the moments sweet.
And sing the old songs o'er again,
Old songs that build the hearts of men.

The town of Whitewater was first known as Hillsboro. Hillsboro was recorded in 1828 and the Whitewater post office was established in 1832. The name of the town was changed to Whitewater in 1850. Although the railroads never came to Whitewater, it had many businesses through the years. The last business was B. F. Wolfe's Garage closing in 1992.

Community life of recent years has centered around the Masonic Lodge, the Whitewater Book Club, the Methodist and Christian Churches and the school. The first Whitewater high school graduation was in 1894. In 1922–1923 the new Whitewater High School was built adding much needed space for the children. A further addition was made in 1954 to the old grade school. A consolidation of Webster, New Garden, Franklin and Green townships was made in 1962, becoming the Northeastern Wayne School Corporation. Whitewater high school students attended Fountain City until the new Northeastern High School was built in 1967. An elementary school remained at Whitewater for a few years. The activity of the Franklin township today centers around the farms and the churches.

A Pictorial History of Wayne County, Indiana

Cross streets in Whitewater on May 30, 1954. Service flags, made by the Ladies Auxiliary of the Franklin Township Conservation Club, were for World War I, World War II and the Korean Conflict. Courtesy of Mrs. B. F. Wolf

Whitewater Ground Observer Tower built in 1952. Although the town had only one hundred twenty-five residents at the time, the tower was manned 24 hours a day with shifts of 4, 6, or 8 hours. Courtesy of Mrs. B. F. Wolfe

The Ray Knoll farm in Franklin Township on Arba Pike. Knoll owned the farm from 1937–1991. Mrs. Knoll is hanging clothes on the line. Her garden is on the left with the grape arbors behind it. Courtesy of Anita Knoll

Whitewater Conservation Club House, 1951. The club sponsored fox drives and stocked pheasants for hunting. It was the site of many community activities. Courtesy of Mrs. B. F. Wolf

The fear of a Soviet nuclear attack on the United States led to an interesting development in Franklin Township. Because of the strategic significance of Wright-Patterson Air Base in defending the United States and the manufacturing plants of Detroit, Air Watchers Towers were placed at various areas within a 100-mile radius of the air base. A tower was set up at Whitewater in 1952. It was manned for a time, twenty-four hours a day in four-hour shifts

Franklin Township has one claim to fame which cannot be disputed, except by some in Randolph County. The highest point in Indiana is located .3 miles south of the Randolph/Wayne County line on Elliott Road. The Highpointers Club and Trail Heads have placed a sign-in book at the location where one can leave messages and observations. An entry of March 3, 1997 reads, "Invaded this high point to return it to its rightful place in Randolph County where it was stolen away by the Rebels in Wayne County. So, next time it will be back in Randolph County where it belongs." Randolph County Highway Department.

This created a puzzle because Wayne County has the official survey high point for Indiana of 1,257 feet at this location. Upon investigation, Randolph County's highest point is 1,200 feet, but because of a huge compacted trash landfill created near Modoc, the highest point is now being disputed by them. It remains to be seen whether the Highpointers Club and Trail Heads will find a landfill as interesting as the climb over the fence into the woods where trees guard a stack of stones marking Indiana's highest spot.

A Pictorial History of Wayne County, Indiana

Frank Wolf's Garage in 1955. His station was in operation until 1992 and was the last business in Whitewater. Courtesy of Mrs. B. F. Wolf

Richard Mullins of Whitewater became one of the country's leading songwriters and singers of Christian Music. His songs were nominated several times for the Dove Award. He was killed in a car accident in September 1997. Courtesy of Richard Lewis

Highest spot in Indiana on the Goble Farm, Elliott Road. Edward Lafever looks at the sign-in book prepared for visitors to the site. Photo by Carolyn Lafever

B. A. Fox General Merchandise and filling station, Williamsburg, circa 1920s. B. A. Fox is in the long apron. Courtesy of Jack Phelps

Chapter 7

Green Township

Green Township was taken from Perry Township except for sections of the east side which came from New Garden. The name is believed to have come either from an early settler named John Green or for John Green, a somewhat notorious Indian. It is believed the Indian Green's name was also given to the Greens Fork River. Stories are told which say he was involved in murder and mayhem and others tell of his operating a tavern near Williamsburg. His influence appears to have been strong among white pioneers for them to name a township for him.

The town of Williamsburg was laid out at the request of William Johnson who settled in Green Township. His will of 1830 directed that one section of his "plantation" be laid out for a town which became Williamsburg, named for him. There were not many places for a traveler or new settler to do business in the northern part of Wayne County and Williamsburg grew to fill that need. It was one of the few settlements between Richmond and Muncie.

In 1900 two turnpikes connected Williamsburg with Richmond and Centerville. Roads through the northern part of the county left much to be desired. The Richmond Free Pike came to Webster and Williamsburg. The road to Economy was filled with twists and turns and eventually turned into the Economy Pike. When a railroad line was proposed in March, 1900 it caused great excitement. It would be good for shipping freight and for passenger travel. The citizens of Green Township anticipated great prosperity.

Rail service to Williamsburg began on June 13, 1901 when the first freight train arrived. The first passenger train arrived on July 2, with a group of Bartels' clerks on an excursion to Osborn

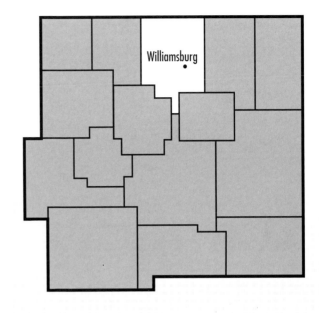

Year formed: 1821

Town: Williamsburg, unincorporated

1990 Township Population: 1,249

Size: 28.5 Square Miles

Waterways: Greens Fork

Topography: Fairly flat, some rolling hills

Main roads: US 35, Centerville Road

Roy Stevens, in the leather apron, stands with a friend in front of his shop in Williamsburg in 1910. Blacksmiths made shoes for the horses, did much iron work and repaired farm tools. Courtesy of Kathryn Williams

Railroad men using a large crane to work on the railroad through Williamsburg on the Chesapeake and Ohio (C&O) Railroad. The railroad was built by the Cincinnati, Richmond and Muncie (CR&M) Railroad, which merged with C&O in 1903. Courtesy of Kathryn Williams

A landmark in Williamsburg, this gigantic loudspeaker broadcast in 1927 for the first radio in town. Made of concrete and sanded to an alabaster-like smoothness, it was nine feet tall with a diameter of thirty inches and weighed six hundred pounds. It could be heard for three miles. Photo by Ed Lafever

A group of school girls from the Williamsburg area about 1914. Their summer dresses show the changing styles of women's clothing as their ankles can be seen. Courtesy of Kathryn Williams

Lake in Economy. People were so excited about the trains that they made special trips to Williamsburg just to see the passenger trains. Seventy-three tickets were sold at Williamsburg for one of the early excursion (special tour) trains which went west to Economy or east to Richmond. Automobiles were still just a dream for the average American and trains filled an important need for good transportation.

On the same day the train made its first stop in Williamsburg, Mr. Kessler started his elevator. The elevator handled the farmers' harvest of corn, oats, and wheat and it also mixed feed for farm animals. Coal was an important fuel and a load could be ordered from the elevator. Elevators served a social purpose for the farmers who could visit and catch up on the news while waiting for the feed to be mixed.

Another business which was to benefit from the new mode of travel was the old Williamsburg Hotel. The hotel was built in the 1840s and became an important place for rail travelers. Train schedules were not dependable and there were

B. A. Fox standing behind the counter of his store in Williamsburg in the 1920s. Courtesy of Jack Phelps

A Pictorial History of Wayne County, Indiana

Williamsburg Elevator owned by James Frazer, circa 1944–1945. The old office is the small building by the car. Courtesy of Kathryn Williams

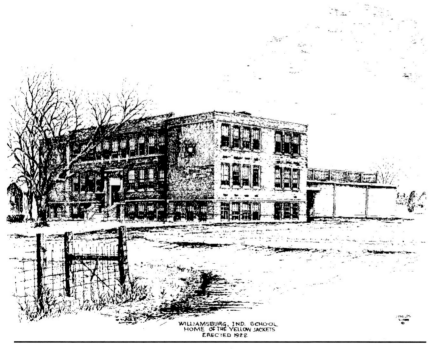

Williamsburg High School, home of the Yellow Jackets sports teams, circa 1965. It became an elementary school from 1972 until the mid-1970s. Drawing by Jack Phelps

Farm and home of Junior and Kathryn Williams, Davis Meyer Road, north of Williamsburg, 1970. The hay elevator stands ready to lift hay bales into the barn. Most hay today is made into round bales instead of the familiar rectangles. Courtesy of Kathryn Williams

many train wrecks in those days which caused delays. Stranded or delayed passengers went to the hotel to be fed and housed. Around 1910 the hotel was purchased by George and Emma Kelley. Their hotel became a popular place for dining. With the advent of automobiles, people of the cities and the surrounding area liked to drive to a good eating place. Large groups of people came to the Kelley hotel from as far as Muncie, Richmond and Winchester.

There were eight township schools built for the children of Green Township. They began to consolidate and the first commencement from the township high school was in 1894. A new Williamsburg school opened in 1923. When Green Township joined with the Northeastern Wayne Unit in 1962, Webster school was closed and the students came to Williamsburg. The last Williamsburg graduation was in 1967 and the school became an elementary. Seven through twelve went to the new Northeastern school at

Oakes' Main Street Market, 1997, a bulk food store in Williamsburg serving many Amish clients who have moved to Wayne County. Photo by Carolyn Lafever

A Pictorial History of Wayne County, Indiana

Artists Doris and Jack Phelps in their studio on W. E. Oler Road. Jack has drawn many historic places in pen and ink. Doris paints animals and abstracts. Both have won awards for their art. Photo by Ed Lafever

Elk on the Deer Creek Farms, Inc. north of Williamsburg. Owner Bill Ingle raises elk and ostriches. Photo by Carolyn Lafever

Students from Earlham College and area high schools came to study the native woods and wild flowers over the years. A classified forest is not state or public property. It is privately owned and one should have permission to explore it.

Radio came to Williamsburg by way of a huge speaker horn. Clifford Duke built a 9 ft. tall loudspeaker in 1927, apparently to share this interesting new media with the town. The huge horn could be heard for up to three miles and was used to broadcast news, baseball games and other things of interest. This was the only radio in town at the time and the horn stood for years until it was given to the Wayne County Museum.

Williamsburg has lost the railroad, elevator, school and many business places. But the Methodist, the Friends and the Nazarene churches remain active. The Lions Club built an activity park and provides support for sports programs. The school gym is still used by the community. In 1975 the population of the township had dropped to about one thousand. By 1990 it had gained about two hundred fifty residents.

Fountain City. When Whitewater school closed, Williamsburg became a double-shifted school for two years. Williamsburg and Webster came from 7 a.m. to 12 p.m. and Whitewater and Fountain City from 12 to 5 p.m. Eventually all the children were able to attend the new Northeastern elementary school.

In 1921 Indiana enacted a Forest land Act, which encouraged farmers to set aside at least three acres or more to support the growth of native or planted woods. This was designated by the state forester as a classified forest, for production of timber, the protection of water-sheds or control of soil erosion. The first in the county was a mile south of Williamsburg on the east side of the Centerville Road. The Lewis Family set aside eighty acres which had never been cut or pastured. It had been in the family since about 1830.

Harvest Land Co-Op on Jacksonburg Road, also known as the Walnut Level Elevator. It started as a Farm Bureau Co-Op in 1958. This is one of four grain elevators left in Wayne County. Nearly all small towns had elevators until railroads closed and new technology took over. Photo by Ed Lafever

Harrison Township

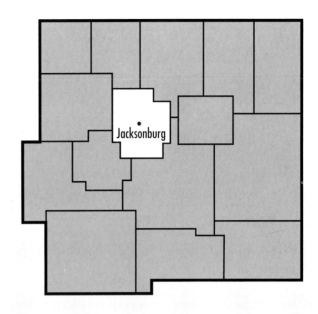

Jacksonburg

When Indiana became a state in 1816, the county commissioners were told to divide the counties into smaller municipal divisions. Wayne County was divided into six townships with Harrison Township one of the first six. Its boundaries were different and it was a larger territory. Harrison Township as it is today was formed and organized in 1843.

The only settlement to reach standing as a village in Harrison Township was Jacksonburg. It was laid out and recorded in 1814, one of the earliest in the county. It was a part of Jackson Township and the polling place until 1836, which was moved to Cambridge City. For a few years Jacksonburg was a central place for military parades, horse racing and other social activities. Several businesses were established such as a tannery, pottery, a hat shop, blacksmith shops and general stores. In the early years of Wayne County, Jacksonburg was an important village and trading post.

The forests surrounding Jacksonburg were mainly walnut trees. As settlers came and cut the timber, fine rich soil was revealed. The flat, fertile land between Greens Fork and Martindale Creek was called Walnut Level. It extended from the north edge of Harrison Township to Washington Township. An early mill along the Whitewater Canal route in Milton was called the Walnut Level Mill. The elevator built by the Farm Bureau Co-op in northern Harrison Township was also called Walnut Level. In the 1840s a hotel in East Germantown was named the Walnut Level House.

When the railroad passed through the township the tracks were laid a few miles north of Jacksonburg. Since the town was not on a main road or railroad it rapidly lost business. There was no depot or official stop but one could flag down

Year formed: 1817; Organized 1843

Town: Jacksonburg, unincorporated

1990 Township Population: 363

Size: 17 Square Miles

Waterways: Greens Fork, Martindale Creek

Topography: Northern flat. Southern slightly rolling.

Main roads: Main roads: Jacksonburg Road, Interstate 70

A Pictorial History of Wayne County, Indiana

Rec'd of Adam Rader $173½ cents his tax in full for the year 1833 By me John Jones Dep col'r D. Led

No. 129 TAX RECEIPT FOR 1861. $49.11

Treasurer's Office, Wayne Co., Ind., Aug 14 1862

Received of Adam Rader the sum of

Forty Nine Dollars and 11 Cts, in full of the Tax assessed for State, Military, County, School, Sinking Fund, School House, Road and Township purposes for the year 1861, on the following property:

Sec	Lot Sun	Block Range	Town Acre	Value, $	Tax $
Aa M2 ARng 17	16	13	110	3578	
S2o Mog 18	16	18	4	152	
N2o SSg 18	16	13	77	2850	
SS Ca NNg 18	16	13	38		49.11
			Road		3.78
					45.33

$938 Personal property and Polls C. B. Huff Treas. Wayne Co.

Two tax receipts, issued to Adam Rader, the first from 1833 for 173-1/2 cents and the second for $49.11, issued in 1862 from the court house in Centerville. Homesteaded in 1819, a descendent of Rader, Firman Riggs still lives there. Courtesy of Firman Riggs

Certificate of Stock.

No. 10

This is to Certify That Adam Rader is the Proprietor of Six Shares of Stock in the Jacksonburg Turnpike Company, which Stock is transferrable only on the books of said Company, by the surrender of this CERTIFICATE.

In Testimony Whereof, The President and Clerk of said Company have hereunto set their hands this 21 day of February 1854

M. D. Leuson Clerk. S. S. Boyd President.

A Certificate of Stock for six shares issued to Adam Rader in 1854 by the Jacksonburg Turnpike Company. First settler Samuel Boyd was the president. Courtesy of Firman Riggs

Old Smokehouse or bee house on Washington at the home of Jabez and Catherine Beeson. This was the original log house, covered with clapboard. Note the root or storm cellar to the right. Courtesy Francis and Pollyanna Ammerman

the train at the railroad crossing on Jacksonburg Road and ride west to Hagerstown or east to Richmond. This flag stop was called Walnut Level. As late as the 1920–1930s, one could flag down the train and catch a ride. The passenger train, with its distinctive whistle, passed through about 11 a.m. in the morning and returned about 5 p.m. The whistles of freight trains were different from passenger trains. According to long time resident, Robert Endsley, Sr., the morning passenger train whistle signaled it was almost time for dinner and the evening whistle told it was time to do the evening chores. A grain elevator was built at the Walnut Level railroad crossing in 1958 and is still a shipping point for the grain harvest of local farmers.

The first white settler, Samuel Boyd, was a minister and the first missionary to bring the "good tidings" into this territory. He traveled on foot and horse-back with his son-in-law, Elijah Martindale, also a noted minister. They estab-

lished churches in Wayne and surrounding counties and preached successfully to the Indians. During the War of 1912, Boyd built a fort for protection of the settlers. In 1815 they organized a "New Light" church in Jacksonburg. The congregation changed its name to Jacksonburg Christian Church in 1839 and is still active today. The early Quakers formed a society in West Union about 1 1/2 miles south of Jacksonburg which lasted about fifteen years.

Harrison Township's four district schools consolidated into one building at Jacksonburg in the late 1800s. The wood frame building was just east of the town. In 1909 a brick building was built on the same site with two large rooms. Four classes were held in each room, grades 1–8. In the early 1950s an addition was added. By 1959 grades 7 and 8 were sent to school at Hagerstown.

When the new school districts were formed in Wayne County, Jacksonburg school became part of the Nettle Creek School Corporation. In

A Pictorial History of Wayne County, Indiana

Olive Beeson and her hunter husband, Rob. Their home was on Washington Road south of Greens Fork. Circa 1905. Courtesy of Francis and Pollyanna Ammerman

The elusive wolf of Walnut Level was shot by Elmer McGrew on April 7, 1920. The "prairie wolf" or coyote made costly raids on farm animals and eluded hunters for several months. When settlers cleared the land, the larger timber wolf moved to the wilderness. The coyote, more solitary than wolves, learned to live with man. Courtesy of Esther Bond

The Jacksonburg School was built in 1909 and used until 1962. Harrison Township consolidated with Nettle Creek School Corporation in 1962. Courtesy of Pollyanna Ammerman

The Jacksonburg grocery store, 1969. The first store in the building was started in 1871. The
Independent Order of Odd Fellows added the second story in 1878. The last owner was Helen Scott
Bright who closed it after a robbery in 1974. Courtesy of Wayne County Historical Museum

1962 a decision was made not to remodel the
school building and it was closed. Harrison
Township students were sent to Hagerstown.
Since there had never been a high school in
Harrison Township, for a few years older children
had the choice of attending Cambridge City,
Greens Fork or Hagerstown, depending on where
they lived. However by 1930 the only school
hack which operated from Harrison went to
Hagerstown.

Since 1883, Dougherty Orchards has produced apples from their orchards in Harrison
Township on a farm owned by the family before
the Civil War. William Henry Dougherty put out
a five-acre peach and apple orchard. There came
a time when the peach orchard was the most
valuable part. Labor Day weekend was the big
"peach day." Peaches were so valuable during the
depression that guards had to be hired to protect
the peach crop. Peaches sold for $5 a bushel, an
enormous price and an easy way for thieves to
make some money.

The Jacksonburg Christian Church celebrated one hundred fifty years in
1989. The congregation was organized by first settler, Samuel Boyd, in
1815. Courtesy of Francis and Pollyanna Ammerman

A Pictorial History of Wayne County, Indiana

Log house, circa 1815–1820 moved to the Dougherty Orchard grounds in 1975. It was given to Joan Dougherty by Raymond Jackson from the Josiah Bundy homestead, circa 1815. Arnold and Ann Dougherty stand in front. Courtesy of Dougherty Orchards

Imago Pepsi, from Pepsi-Land Horse Farm on Jacksonburg Road, is owned by Diana Keiser and ridden by jockey Duane Keiser. He has just won a purse of $49,577.25 at Mount Pleasant, Michigan, 1988. Duane was leading jockey of Indiana in 1974, winning the most races in Indiana. Courtesy of Diana and Duane Keiser

One of the treats in the fall was to go to the orchard for winter apples to be stored in cellar. Apples were special treats at Christmas and with popcorn was a "snack food" of choice long before modern day chips appeared. The Doughterty family still operates the orchard business and have added new attractions. They include a petting farm and lake which opened in 1992 and Doughtery's McMaze, a corn-field maze shaped into the state of Indiana in 1996.

Harrison Township is almost totally rural with a few residents in Jacksonburg. The last store closed in 1974. A radiator and welding shop occupies the old school building. When Interstate 70 was built in 1962 through the center of the township two new businesses were added, Gas America and McDonalds restaurant at the I-70, State Road 1 exit. Community life in Harrison Township had centered around the Christian church, the school and the Odd Fellows Lodge. The school closed, the lodge merged with Greens Fork, and of the three centers only the church is left. Township residents support school activities, business and events in nearby towns.

Martindale State Fishing Area. A quiet country fishing lake just east of Jacksonburg. It was created when fill dirt was needed for nearby I-70. Photo by Ed Lafever

Interurban stopped in Cambridge City, circa 1905. The track which divides and goes to the right (south) was for the "Dinky" to Milton.

Courtesy of Jack Phelps

Chapter 8

Jackson Township

The *Cambridge City Tribune* of March 1911 describes how things were in Cambridge City. "There are Public Utilities, the Common School, a Commissioned High School, Water Works, Electric Light Plant, Fire Department, two cemeteries, 25 acres of Park Ground, 30 miles of Macadamized Streets (a type of crushed stone), 15 miles of cement walks, no Saloons, no Blind Tigers, No Gambling, Rich Soil Beneath, the Blue Sky above."

Cambridge City is one of the four incorporated towns in Jackson Township. The township was formed in 1817 as one of the first six in Wayne County. Its voting center for many years was Jacksonburg. Jackson Township originally contained about sixty square miles, but the formation of Center Township shortly after and Harrison in 1843 reduced its area to 28 1/2 square miles. The first settlers came in 1809 and settled south of East Germantown. Carolina Quakers and Pennsylvania Germans were the principal first inhabitants. The Quakers came first and the German element began to arrive about 1820.

The first town to be platted in Jackson was Georgetown in 1827. It was populated by several German families and by 1832 its had become Germantown. The "East" was added later to distinguish it from another place in Indiana called Germantown. The town grew because it was a "ribbon city" built along the National Road. Travelers found deep ruts and mud on the Road of the 1830s. They could travel only a few miles a day, requiring many places to stop for refreshment and rest. There were many inns in and near Germantown. When the railroad came through in the 1850s, National Road travel slowed somewhat and there was less need for inns. Those remaining were mostly in the towns.

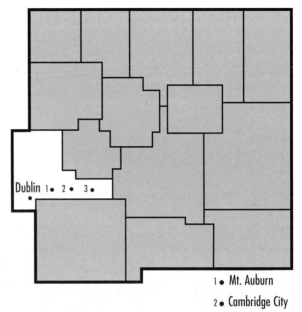

Year formed: 1817

1 ● Mt. Auburn
2 ● Cambridge City
3 ● East Germantown

Town: Cambridge City, East Germantown, Dublin, Mount Auburn

1990 Township Population: 4,803

Size: 28 1/2 Square Miles

Waterways: West Fork of Whitewater River, Symonds Creed, Martindale Creek

Topography: Undulating and somewhat hilly

Main roads: U.S. 40, Indiana 1

A Pictorial History of Wayne County, Indiana

Oscar Jameson at his home on East Main Street in East Germantown, 1917. Oscar sold Shinola shoe polish for miles around by traveling on the interurban, the railroad and in this fine truck. His hobby was photography and he took many pictures of his home town.
 Courtesy of Dan Poole

The Walnut Level House in East Germantown built between 1833–1840. It was a hotel and the I.O.O.F. lodge used the third floor. It burned in 1904. Courtesy of Cambridge City Library

The Coffee Pot Restaurant, a familiar sight along U.S. 40 for many years. It stood in what was known as Pennville, twelve miles west of Richmond. It was destroyed by fire. Courtesy of Cambridge City Library

The Kocher Building in 1935 in East Germantown. D. W. and Mabel Kocher started their business in 1913. The interurban tracks shown in the street were covered over when the road was resurfaced. The interurban was discontinued in 1931. Courtesy of Dan Poole

By 1883 East Germantown was prosperous enough to incorporate. There were several stores, at least two hotels, a lodge, some factories and one of the oldest Lutheran congregations in continuous existence in Indiana. Zion's Lutheran Church was established in 1822. The town had its own elementary school for many years until the consolidation in 1962. The East Germantown School is now the Western Wayne School Corporation administration office.

When World War I started in 1914, Americans tried to stay neutral but opinion was divided about which side they should support. Since Germany was the aggressor and eventually was responsible for many American deaths, sentiment ran high against anyone of German origin. A move was made to change the name of East Germantown to Pershing, to honor General John J. Pershing, commander of the American forces in Europe. A petition was sent to the Post Office Department requesting to change the post office name to Pershing. The request was granted but the town name was not officially changed. In February, 1920 a special election was held to decide whether the corporate name of the town should be changed to Pershing. The vote was 38-32 in favor of keeping the name of East Germantown. Some still call the town Pershing, causing confusion to this day. The town limit signs on U.S. 40 list both names.

As one travels west on U.S. 40 from East Germantown, the next town is Cambridge City. It was platted in 1836 as Cambridge and soon became an important port on the Whitewater Canal. The word "City" was added in 1864 to prevent confusion with another Indiana town of the same name. The town was laid out with growth in mind. Space was allotted for market areas on both

A Pictorial History of Wayne County, Indiana

East Germantown's Zion's Lutheran Church, built in 1900. It is the oldest Lutheran congregation in Indiana in continuous existence. Courtesy of Phyllis Mattheis

West shore of Lake Wehi, south of East Germantown. From the 1930s to 1950s this was a recreation area for swimming, boating, dances and boxing matches. The name WEHI is from the first letter of the first names of its developers, William Dwyer, Edwin Wickes, Hilbert Jones, and Irvin Harmeier. Courtesy of Jack Phelps

Imperial Mills, Cambridge City, about 1900, owned by William Creitz. This was one of the largest flouring mills in the nation. Creitz donated land which is now the Creitz Park for Cambridge City's children. Courtesy of Wayne Bank

A picture on a Christmas card from 1909–1910. The message read, "Ten years ago Rural Route No. 14 was established. In this time the associations between the carrier and patrons have been very pleasant.... I am Your Humble Carrier, Moses T. Shideler." Courtesy of Blanche Fuson

the east and west sides of the river. Canal basins were laid out near the proposed canal site and there was space for warehouses which would be built beside the basins. The streets were wide in anticipation of the traffic along the National Road and commerce from the canal. Church Street was a long canal basin extending to the river with narrow streets on either side.

For a few short years the Whitewater Canal did bring prosperity to the area. The last load of flour on the canal from Hagerstown to Cincinnati was in 1855. Although the canal failed, railroads helped to save the towns. In the 1850s a train system took over most of the east-west traffic. In the late 1860s, the canal tow path had become the Big Four railroad for north-south traffic. In 1910 the Pennsylvania Railroad elevated the tracks through Cambridge City to ease the steep grade between it and Dublin. This work brought new people to the area and many of them came to stay.

Cambridge City continued to prosper and to make improvements. In 1914 Richmond's *Evening Item* gave recognition to the town when it stated, "Cambridge City, our industrious and wide awake little neighbor to the west, now has the distinction of being the best lighted city in Wayne County." The newspaper went on to describe Richmond as being "second class" as far as lighting was concerned. The article refers to the thirty new cluster lights which adorned the streets of Cambridge City. The funds were raised by the community at practically no cost to the city. Buckskin Ben, A Wild West showman whose home base was in Cambridge City, gave a benefit performance for the Cluster Light Fund in 1914. The cluster lights were used until the 1950s when tall trucks broke off or damaged the cluster arms and globes. Finally the remaining clusters were removed and new lights were installed.

A Pictorial History of Wayne County, Indiana

Main Street in Cambridge City, circa 1915, looking south on Green Street. The new cluster lighting system was considered the best in Wayne County. Tall trucks damaged the cluster lights which had to be removed in the 1950s. Courtesy of Wayne Bank

Cambridge City's cheese factory. The wagon load of cheese is ready to be shipped on the train. Mr. Grey, the cheese maker, is wearing the apron. James Boyd and George Drischel sit on the cheese wagon. Courtesy of Wayne Bank

Gaar Nursery, Cambridge City. A field of shrubs east of Cambridge City. Milton H. Gaar, founder, is on the left. Homer Howell, right, worked at the nursery, circa 1925. The Gaar Nursery is presently located west of Dublin. Courtesy of Jim Brower

The Lackey Horse sales from 1888–1913 brought buyers to Cambridge City from around the nation and from foreign countries. This was the center of an Indiana horse industry and the Lackey sale became known for the fine horses sold through it. A horse sold in the 1912 sale became the world-famous pacer, Single G. The unruly two-year-old came from the L. D. Commons farm in Centerville. The horse was bought by W. B. Barefoot of Cambridge City, who already was part owner of the horse and realized his potential. Barefoot's expert trainers worked with the horse and he began racing as a three-year-old. Single G's remarkable history of winning races was honored in 1950 by leading horsemen and admirers of fine horses. He was voted the greatest pacer of the first half of the twentieth century.

In 1911, four sisters established the Overbeck Pottery at their home in Cambridge City. From its earliest days Overbeck Pottery gained honors. It won awards in art shows in Indiana, across the United States and in interna-

tional exhibits. In recent years pottery and art produced by the Overbeck sisters has become highly valued by collectors of the American Arts and Crafts style. It has earned an important place in the history of American art. Kathleen and Arthur Postle presented their Overbeck collection to the Cambridge City Library and an Overbeck Museum was established there.

In 1846 a huge flour mill was built by Benjamin Conklin. William Creitz operated it from 1889–1929 when it was one of the largest and most prosperous mills in the nation. It was known as the Imperial Mill. In 1908 Mr. Creitz gave twenty-four acres to the city for a park which was named for him. The park is located south and west of the high school.

General Solomon Meredith and his three sons all served in the Civil War. From 1834 he served in many official offices: Sheriff of Wayne County, Representative in the Indiana Legislature, U.S. Marshal for Indiana and Clerk of Wayne County. In 1861 he was appointed a colonel of the

Cambridge City home of Mr. & Mrs. Franklin Reynolds, owner of the Standard Mfg. Co.,1930s. Mrs. Reynolds served as Indiana State Treasurer, 1926–1931. She was the first woman elected to a major office in Indiana and the first woman elected to a state treasurer's office in the nation. Courtesy of Jim Brower

Advertising picture of a chair manufactured by the Standard Mfg. Co. of Cambridge City. The weight of the chair is 7 1/4 lb.,the weight of the people is 1033 lb. Top: Louise Gray and Russell Stickler; Center: William Oldman, M.S. Bowmaster and Clifford Oldman. Frank Carper sits on the chair. Courtesy of Cambridge City Library

Cambridge City Main Street in 1929. The arrow points to an early location of the Wayne Trust Company, which today is the Wayne Bank and Trust Co. Today the home office is across the street. It is the oldest family owned bank in Indiana. Courtesy of Wayne Bank

Overbeck House and Studio on E. Church Street. Phyllis Mattheis stands by the marker. She and her husband, Jerry, restored the residence. It was placed on the National Register of Historic Places in 1976. Courtesy of Phyllis Mattheis

19th Regular Indiana Volunteer Infantry, part of the famous "Iron Brigade." His home has been restored and is privately owned.

Mount Auburn is another small town built along the National Road in 1864. It was the last of the four towns to be platted and is sandwiched between Cambridge City and Dublin. It is home to the Huddleston Farmhouse Museum Inn, a house and inn built in the 1840s. Most of Mount Auburn lies to the north of the old Road which is now U.S. 40.

Dublin is on the west side of Jackson Township and its limits extend almost to the Henry County line. It was platted in 1830 and grew nearly as much as Cambridge City in its early days. The canal and the railroads gave Cambridge City an edge and in 1917 Dublin relinquished its high school to Cambridge City. There have been many businesses in Dublin such as the Wayne Agricultural Works. The foundry was opened in 1837 and built farm equipment. In 1875 it came under new ownership, became known as Wayne Works and was moved to Richmond.

The Golay Community Center was presented to the people of the Western Wayne area in 1981. It was a gift from the Charles R. Golay family. Golay & Co., Inc. was the largest manufacturing firm in Cambridge City for several years. Photo by Carolyn Lafever

Lakeview Restaurant in Mount Auburn, a favorite dining spot for residents of Wayne County since the 1940s. Windows overlook a lake which is home to wild ducks and geese. Photo by Carolyn Lafever

The Huddleston Farmhouse Inn Museum in Mount Auburn. John Huddleston moved into the house in the 1840s. It was an early inn on the Old National Road. Photo by Carolyn Lafever

G. W. Murray Drug Store. The I.O.O.F. lodge building is on the right. Dublin, circa 1910. Courtesy of Dublin Library

The Double-Inn Tavern, circa 1890s, on the National Road in Dublin. It was partly demolished by the townspeople of Dublin when its proprietor, Loren Custer tried to sell whiskey in the tavern. Courtesy of Dublin Library

The origin of Dublin's name remains a mystery, but some have credited it to the old "Double-Inn Tavern" which had two entrances. Other stories tell about the long hill on the National Road from Cambridge City to Dublin. It took two teams of horses or oxen to pull up the heavy wagons, thus having to "double up." In later years a spare railroad engine was kept at Cambridge City to help pull freight trains up the steep grade. The elevating of the railroad in 1910 considerably lowered the grade between the two towns.

Jackson Township is not all towns, although with four along U.S. 40 it might seem so. There are many prosperous farms and country homes in the township. All of the children now attend school in Cambridge City as a part of the Western Wayne School Corporation. Cambridge City and Dublin have their own libraries and fire departments. The residents of each of the towns and surrounding areas have a high interest in their churches, their children and the well-being of their respective communities. Western Wayne Heritage, Inc. offers tours occasionally for visitors to see the historic buildings in the area. This is one of Wayne County's most diverse and well maintained historic areas.

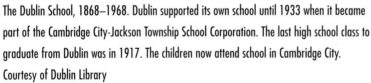

The Dublin School, 1868–1968. Dublin supported its own school until 1933 when it became part of the Cambridge City-Jackson Township School Corporation. The last high school class to graduate from Dublin was in 1917. The children now attend school in Cambridge City. Courtesy of Dublin Library

Henley's Grocery Store, 1916, stood where the Dublin City Building is located. Courtesy of Dorothy Wissler

Dublin has had a town library since 1859. After fire destroyed most of it, a new library was organized in 1884, located at the school. This building was remodeled and opened in 1943. Courtesy of Dublin Library

Fun Festival Parade, 1954. The Perfect Circle band rides in a truck provided by the Hagerstown Lumber Company. The lumber company and the grain elevator burned in 1958 about five days apart and were believed to have been arson fires. Courtesy of Jason Schmittler

Chapter 9

Jefferson Township

In 1809, territory was procured from the Indians which was called the Twelve Mile Purchase. The Purchase added area to Wayne County and the west boundary runs through the center of Jefferson Township. Land on the east side was for sale from the Federal Government in 1811. It was not until 1818 that land on the west side of the line could be bought. People had already settled there. When the land was for sale, some could not afford to buy the farms they had carved out of the forest.

About 1822 Jefferson Township began to grow in population. The town of Hagerstown was platted in 1832. By 1834 enough people lived in the community to want their own township. Jefferson was formed from Jackson on the south and Perry on the north. Religious groups had organized as early as 1816, with Salem Baptist Church being first. The congregation still meets in the little country church on Salem Church Road.

In 1820 a group with strong religious convictions settled in the Nettle Creek valley near Hagerstown. German Baptist or Dunkards, had come to the United States from Germany after enduring much persecution in the 1700s. The group which settled in Jefferson Township migrated from Pennsylvania to Ohio and eventually into Wayne County. The Nettle Creek Church congregation formed in 1820, meeting at homes until a large brick church was built in 1844–1845. The German Baptists wore distinctive dark clothing similar to the Quakers. The congregation grew so large that several chapels were built to accommodate members living farther away. In 1874 a second brick structure replaced the first. The church is known as the "Brick Church." A new sanctuary was built in

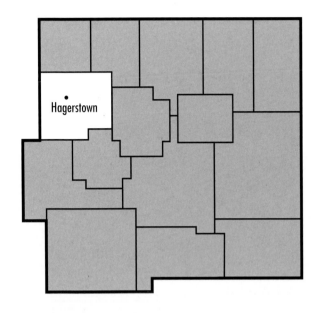

Year formed: 1834

Town: Hagerstown

1990 Township Population: 3,331

Size: 28 square miles

Waterways: Nettle Creek, West Fork of Whitewater River, Martindale Creek

Topography: Mostly rolling, some hilly

Main roads: Indiana 1, Indiana 38

A Pictorial History of Wayne County, Indiana

E. B. Reynolds of Hagerstown, right with beard, with Sioux Indians in council at Standing Rock, S.D. in 1891. They are asking for payment for ponies taken from them in 1876 by white soldiers. Reynolds was a special Indian agent who helped settle problems for the Indians. Courtesy of Leon Reynolds

William Wedekind, World Champion Horse Shoer, Hagerstown. The award was given at the World's Fair in Chicago, 1893. His blacksmith shop was in Hagerstown and his award-winning display is in the Wayne County Museum. Collection of Carolyn Lafever

Two-seated, pedaled Light Inspection Car, circa 1900, invented by Charles N. Teetor. The business eventually became Perfect Circle Corporation in Hagerstown. Courtesy of Jason Schmittler

Hagerstown Fair grounds, circa 1905. The horse racing track attracted many fair-goers and helped end the Dalton Fair. It was located at the site of the high school football field. The GHKC on the judges stand advertises for the George H. Knollenberg Company in Richmond. Collection of Carolyn Lafever

The 5¢ Theater, Hagerstown Main Street, circa 1912. The morning after Halloween pranksters played their tricks. The old clapboard buildings burned in the fire of 1969, destroying all the buildings west of Beachler's Furniture on the south side of Main Street. From the collection of Carolyn Lafever

1967–1968 which was connected to the older building. Their distinctive style of dress changed in the 1920–1930s and only the women occasionally wear prayer bonnets. The Brick Church, now the Nettle Creek Church of the Brethren, is located west of town on Brick Church Road.

The German Baptists were intelligent, innovative and hard working people. They farmed, built mills and started other businesses. The Teetor family, later known for the Perfect Circle Company, came with this group. Their relative, Lewis Teetor, was an elder for the Brick Church for more than fifty years. He wrote a commentary on the New Testament and for twenty years was a trustee for Manchester College.

In 1847 the final eight miles of the Whitewater Canal was completed from Hagerstown to Cambridge City. Hagerstown had formed its own company to finish the canal when it was stopped at Cambridge City. Flooding was a problem south on the canal so the canal engineer built Hagerstown's section on the west side

of the valley. It was several feet higher than the level of the stream. Because of the higher elevation, there was almost no flood damage to Hagerstown's end of the canal. However farther south, flood waters damaged the canal in 1847 and again in 1865. The costly repairs and poor return on investments caused the canal to go out of business.

The Big Four Railroad built on the old towpath of the old canal with the terminus at Hagerstown. A turntable and engine house for the railroad were at the south end of town on Washington Street. Passenger service was discontinued in the 1920s but freight service on the Big Four continued until 1931. The Pennsylvania railroad line from Chicago to Cincinnati also came through Hagerstown and the line now is called the Norfolk Southern Railway.

A Pictorial History of Wayne County, Indiana

Will Abbott, left, stands in front of the New Hindman Hotel on Hagerstown's Main Street, 1908. A fair poster is on the left. Abbott's restaurant was in the hotel where he developed his candy business. Abbott's Candy is the oldest business in Hagerstown, started in the 1890s. Courtesy of the Indiana Historical Society

Phil Haisley's Barber Shop, 1932. Haisley stands at the left and Guy Wilkerson stands behind the young girl waiting for her haircut. Courtesy of Priscilla Haisley

Blanch Fuson and her daughters beside the old spring house. The Fusons moved to their farm on Jacksonburg Road in 1937. Mrs. Fuson, 95, was highly regarded for her angel food cakes, home-made noodles and fresh chicken and eggs. Courtesy of Blanche Fuson

O. F. Smith Poultry Farm, 1941. Letters were staked out with binder twine and chicken feed was placed inside. The photo was taken while the chickens were feeding and it was published in many farm and poultry magazines. Courtesy of Horace Smith

A Christmas greeting in the 1941 December issue of The Circle Magazine. The men are Perfect Circle executives and represents the second generation of Teetors to operate the business. Collection of Carolyn Lafever

In 1895 a new Hagerstown business was organized, the Railway Cycle Manufacturing Company. Charles N. Teetor invented a "railway cycle" which became the Light Inspection Car for inspecting railroad tracks. Later the company (Teetor-Hartley Motor Company, 1914) manufactured automobile motors. They produced many engines for Indiana car makers and the Auburn was their largest customer. The company sold the motor division but kept the growing business of piston rings. In October 1926, the name was changed to the Perfect Circle Company. It became one of the largest piston ring manufacturers in the world.

Charles N. Teetor and his brothers were leaders in the early automotive industry. C. N. Teetor's nephew, Ralph, continued to invent new products for the company such as the Speedostat. The most remarkable part of Ralph's story is that he lost his sight when he was five years old. But blindness did not keep him from a brilliant automotive engineering career. C. N. Teetor died in 1937 and Ralph died in 1982. Perfect Circle was sold to Dana Corporation in 1963 and the Hagerstown facility closed in 1995.

A Pictorial History of Wayne County, Indiana

Ted Sedgwick, left in white shop coat, with students in 1956. Sedgwick's shop classes were popular for the thirty-nine years he taught at Hagerstown. Photo by Lewis Beeson

Hagerstown Airport at the south end of Washington Street, built in 1957–1958. The first airstrip was on the south side of Main Street, east of town. Courtesy of Jason Schmittler

Bob Beeson, left, Sesquicentennial Chairman, explains the plans to Howard Caldwell and Reba Beeson, 1982. Hagerstown Exponent Photo

The Teetors' factory brought many good jobs. Youngsters graduating from high school could work in the factory right at home. During the 1930s depression, Perfect Circle shortened work hours to keep as many employees as possible receiving a paycheck. Perfect Circle was generous to the town and to the area. They gave money to the school, for the public library, and provided machines and tools for the high school Industrial Arts classes. In 1956 Perfect Circle gave a large donation to Cambridge City for their new gymnasium.

Camp Wapi-Kamigi, a woods and lake property south of town, was acquired for the Hagerstown Girl Scouts with the help of Ralph and Nellie Teetor. Summer camps for Girl Scouts of the Treaty Line Council were held there until it closed in 1995. Boy Scouts started in Hagerstown in 1912. Merton Grills, one of the early Scout-masters, set up a college scholarship fund for students graduating from Hagerstown and Cambridge City schools.

There are many interesting characters in Hagerstown's past. Johnnie Horine was known as the "globe-trotting bootblack." Johnnie shined shoes and saved his small earnings for his world travels. He traveled to the Middle East and the Holy Land in 1925 and attended every World Exposition from the 1890s. Johnnie started his trips on his lucky day, June 21, the longest day of the year. Ted Sedgwick was another memorable person. He worked with the Boy Scouts in Hagerstown for thirty years. Sedgwick is fondly remembered for his patient teaching by students who took shop classes during his thirty-nine years at the high school.

Hagerstown's first newspaper was published in 1852. The *Hagerstown Exponent,* the current weekly, was started in 1875. Exponent Publishers was organized in 1969 with the newspaper as one division of it. In 1986 the newspaper was sold to Pat and Bob Hansen. There have been five *Exponent* editors, H. J. Day 1876–1916, Harry Stoltz 1916–1931, Edwin O'Neel 1931–1969, Floyd Lacy 1969–1986, and Bob Hansen, the present editor.

A Pictorial History of Wayne County, Indiana

Nettle Creek Players Tent at the corner of Main and South Plum. The last year shows were played in the tent was 1996. Hagerstown Exponent Photo

Perfect Circle's popular Singing Secretaries performed in Washington, D.C. for the Indiana delegation to the inauguration of President Eisenhour, January 1957. Phil Gates directs. Courtesy of Lewis Beeson

For about twenty-five years a tent theater was set up across the street from Welliver's Restaurant. The Nettle Creek Players gave live productions during the summer with the help of local actors and young professionals. Through the years the theater had difficulty in maintaining itself even with the help of local supporters. The last season for the tent was 1996 and its future is uncertain. For many years Nettle Creek Players presented fine family entertainment on Main Street.

In 1962, Harrison, Clay, Perry, Dalton, Jefferson and half of Liberty Township in Henry County consolidated into the Nettle Creek School Corporation. A new elementary school in Hagerstown was completed in 1968 and the high school on Baker Road in 1971.

Hagerstown has a five-member police department and a volunteer fire department. Historic Hagerstown formed in 1974 and purchased the three-story I.O.O.F building at the corner of Main and Perry streets. They established a museum on the two top floors, continuing to rent business space at the street level. The second floor auditorium is decorated with murals painted in 1913 by local artist, Charles Newcomb. The large room held the school graduations from 1882–1922. It was used for plays, dances, concerts and as a skating rink. In 1982 the town celebrated one hundred fifty years. People from all over the township and beyond served on committees and helped with the celebration.

About half of the population of Jefferson Township lives in the Hagerstown area. Many new homes are being built outside the corporation as farm lands are being divided for housing. A new large elevator was built south of town and the Nettle Creek/I-70 Industrial Park is planned close by. A water tower has been erected and sewer lines have been installed to accommodate the expected industrial growth. Jefferson Township has some of the best farming ground in Wayne County and there are still a few homestead farms which have remained in the families of early settlers.

Hagerstown is best known for Perfect Circle, Tedco, Welliver's Restaurant, the Nettle Creek Players and Abbott's Candy. Several new shops and restaurants have opened downtown in the past few years. The Library built an addition in 1989 and the new city building was built in 1992. Hagerstown's Hometown Christmas has become an annual event which includes a Sunday evening tour of Jefferson Township churches.

Fountain City School basketball team, 1922–1923. Left to right: Carl Showalter, L. W. Smith, John Pegg, Arnold Thomas, Harry Evans, Forrest Hatfield, Roy Miller, Carl Demaree. Courtesy of Jack Phelps

Chapter 10

New Garden Township

Early settlers in New Garden Township were Quakers from the New Garden Meeting in Guilford Township, N.C. This accounts for the name given to the township. The settlers came in 1809–1810 when the area was still the hunting ground for Miami, Delaware, Shawnee and Wyandote Indians. The Indian war of 1812–1814 caused settlers to seek refuge in a blockhouse near Richmond.

Quakers or Friends would not participate in war when it meant they must draw arms against people. They were friendly to Indians, opposed to slavery and honest in their dealings. Friends were immediately recognized by their clothing and for the style of hat worn by the men. Many stories have been told of Quakers being protected because Indians recognized them and left them alone. At the close of the conflict with the Indians in 1814, Obadiah Harris, a settler who had taken refuge at the blockhouse, asked an Indian if he ever saw him when passing by. The Indian replied that he had been seen many times. When asked why he wasn't attacked the Indian said "Son of Penn, Quaker, no shoot."

New Garden Township was one of the first six townships formed when the county was divided in 1816–1817. It included the area of Franklin Township. There were two villages in the township, New Liberty and Newport, now Fountain City. New Liberty, also called New Liberties or West Liberty, was settled by people who did not agree with the anti-slavery ideas of the citizens of Newport. Newport was platted in 1818 and New Liberty in 1820. For a few years New Liberty seemed to grow, but little was heard of it after 1836.

About 1840, Levi and Catharine Coffin began to harbor runaway slaves in their home in Newport. They aided slaves on their way to freedom for about ten years before they moved to Cincinnati. Their

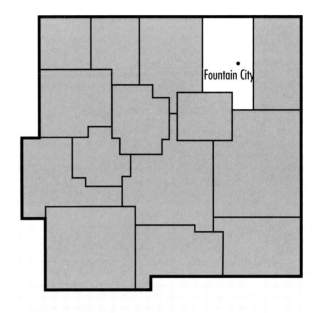

Fountain City

Year formed: 1817

Town: Fountain City

1990 Township Population: 1,847

Size: 24 Square Miles

Waterways: Noland's Fork

Topography: Fairly level with some gently rolling areas

Main roads: U.S. 27 and Fountain City Pike

A Pictorial History of Wayne County, Indiana

The home of Levi Coffin is an Indiana Historic Landmark, commemorating the work of Coffin and others who aided black fugitive slaves from the 1840s through the Civil War. The Coffin House restoration was completed in 1970. Courtesy of the Levi Coffin House

New Garden Friends Church, organized in 1811, the second Friends Meeting in Wayne County. New Garden Township's first settlers were Quakers from North Carolina. The present building was built in 1858 and has been upgraded several times. Courtesy of the Mary C. Sample

Civil War Veterans who lived in Fountain City taken about 1890. The black man in the back row is W. H. Evens. Many blacks settled in New Garden Township after the Civil War because of the good will shown to them by people who had worked for years against slavery. Courtesy of Dave Himelick

Fountain Citys' Main Street looking west, 1905. The town had telephone service and kerosene lamps stood on the street corners. Courtesy of Jack Phelps

activity was part of the escape network for fugitive slaves known as the Underground Railroad. Levi was known as its "conductor." They moved to Cincinnati to operate a free labor store (products produced without slave labor) and to raise funds to help the slaves. Newport (Fountain City) became famous for the work of Coffin and others who gave aid to as many as three thousand slaves before and during the Civil War. After the war, Coffin wrote his memoirs which helped to keep the story of the Underground Railroad alive. Although the Coffins no longer owned the house in Newport, its new owners kept the name and retold the story.

In 1966 the Coffin House was placed on the National Register of Historic Landmarks. The house was purchased by the state of Indiana in 1967. It is operated as a historic house museum by the Levi Coffin House Association and each year hundreds of visitors come to tour the house.

There were other religious groups who felt as strongly about slavery as the Friends. The Society of Wesleyan Methodists at Newport was one of the foremost antislavery organizations in America. The

George G. Williams Blacksmith Shop in Fountain City. Williams stands on the right with a leather apron. The date above the window is 1902. Note the large kerosene light on the corner of the building and the hitching rail at the side. Courtesy of Saundra Jackson

A Pictorial History of Wayne County, Indiana

Fountain City School. Three different schools were built in Fountain City, the last in 1900. It was the first commissioned high school in the state. A gymnasium-auditorium is shown being built about 1924. The last class to graduate was in 1967 and it was razed in 1971. Courtesy of Dave Thomas

The Curry Transfer Company. A push-cart freight service operated by former slave, Wade Curry. He is at the Fountain City Depot waiting for a customer. His badge was only honorary. Courtesy of Dave Thomas

C. N. Hatfield was known for his seed and grain cleaning machines in Fountain City, circa 1905. Courtesy of Dave Thomas

R. C. McNutt Bus Line from Fountain City to Richmond, circa 1930s. The bus description: "it is of the sedan type and finely finished throughout. It has a Studebaker chassis made at South Bend, and a Miller Body made at Defiance, Ohio. The interior is upholstered with leather and it is a might fine vehicle." Courtesy of Dave Himelick

Inventor Charles Francis Jenkins transmitted this visual imaged via what was then called Short Wave Radio. His is known as the "father of the motion picture," and operated the first experimental television station in 1928. This picture was transmitted in 1923 and the label was written by Jenkins. Courtesy of the Wayne County Museum

Wesleyans separated from the Methodists on this issue and the congregation was organized in 1843. The first church was on West Main in Fountain City. The congregation has outgrown its facility several times and a new building was dedicated on U.S. 27 south of town in 1996. It is unusual for such an old congregation to remain stable and grow as large as this church.

In pre-Civil War days, Newport was an island of refuge for black people in a sea of prejudice. They were allowed to engage in business pursuits on an equal basis with white people. This was contrary to the norm for Indiana towns. Before the Civil War Indiana prohibited black immigration to the state, they could not vote, attend public school or testify in court against white people. But the strong anti-slavery sentiment in Newport allowed freed slaves to settle and make a living for themselves.

After the Civil War, several black families made New Garden their home. The rise of the Ku Klux Klan in the 1920s and the depression of the 1930s brought about the move of many blacks from the community. Black families who had worked hard to bring up their children with proper education and an industrious outlook on life found their children unable to find jobs in the area. They were forced to leave Fountain City for Muncie, Dayton, Ohio and farther where higher paying jobs were available for blacks.

Times were prosperous for New Garden Township at the turn of the century. Newport's name was changed to Fountain City in 1878 because there was another Newport in Indiana. The name was chosen because of all the springs, or fountains as they were referred to, that existed in the town at that time. Electric lights came to Fountain City in 1921 and in 1933 Main Street was paved. Fountain City has no traffic light, only a caution light. One older resident told the story that there once was a traffic light in town on a pole in the center of the street. A drunk driver came by late one night and crashed into it. It was decided by the city authorities not to replace the light and since then there has been a yellow caution light on U.S. 27 and a red stop light on Main.

Rupe's Barber Shop in Fountain City in 1964. This was a good place to catch up on the news around town. Courtesy of Saundra Jackson

Ross and Plankenhorn's Texaco Station in Fountain City, 1964, advertised in the school yearbook. Gas prices were 29 cents for Fire Chief and 33 cents for Sky Chief. Courtesy of Saundra Jackson

Preparing for Levi Coffin House tours. Left to Right: Francis Williams, Dave Himelick, Norma Himelick, and Mary Williams. Jeff Himelick is in the old school hack. There has been a continued effort by the community to promote and care for the museum. Courtesy of Francis and Mary Williams

Inventor C. Francis Jenkins was born on a farm in New Garden Township in 1868. He attended Fountain City High School and Earlham College. After spending time in Mexico, he began his inventing career. In 1890 Jenkins went to Washington, D.C. to serve as a secretary at the United States Life Saving Service. In 1894 he invented the first moving picture machine and projector. He set up the Jenkins Laboratories at Washington, D. C. where he invented "Radio-Vision" in 1921 for the purpose of entertaining people at home by showing old movies. His inventions were the forerunners of our present day television. He had over four hundred domestic and international patents in his name. Jenkins died in 1934.

New Garden Township has many farms and threshing rings were an important part of the harvest process. The Meyers Brothers, Russell and Howard, provided equipment for several threshing rings including ones north and south of Williamsburg, west and south of Fountain City.

Threshing rings were formed by neighboring farmers who could not afford their own threshing machines. They shared the rent on the equipment, taking it from farm to farm as the crops were ready to harvest. The women cooked a large dinner at noon for the men and boys on harvest day. The Meyers Brothers operated from about 1920 to 1939. The modern combine has taken the place of the old fashioned threshing rings.

In 1962 Northeastern Wayne School Corporation consolidated the townships of Webster, Green, New Garden and Franklin. A location in New Garden Township, south of Fountain City was chosen for the new school complex. The high school was built first and the other schools were used by grades 1-6 until a new elementary addition was built.

In 1956 the Peoples State Bank was robbed and bank employee Lawrence Strickler was wounded. The robbery was discovered by townspeople who chased the thief. He was quickly apprehended

A Pictorial History of Wayne County, Indiana

Business owners of Fountain City shown in the 1984 Sesquicentennial history book. The oldest business still operating is the Smith McQuiston Funeral Home, serving the area since 1886. Courtesy of Anna K. Mitchell

A joint venture between Fountain City and New Garden Township was completed in 1976. The town and township office building, community hall and fire station were built on the site of the former Fountain City School. Photo by Carolyn Lafever

Walnut Lawn Farm owned by Lillian Mikesell, was homesteaded in 1816 by Jacob Hampton. Mrs. Mikesell is the fifth generation to own it. The log cabin, left, was the first house built at the site. A second house was built with a connecting vestibule. In 1948 the log house was removed. Courtesy of Lillian Mikesell

and the money returned. Five years later in 1961 a disastrous fire destroyed several buildings on the southwest corner of Main and Main Cross Streets. Another shock to the community came in 1970 when Donald R. Goodwin and his brother-in-law, William "Pete" Peters were shot and killed. They had served Fountain City as part-time town marshals. The men were investigating a burglary of the Clyde Hinshaw home late Saturday night on June 6. They apprehended two men, but while interrogating the suspects, the marshals were shot and killed. The assailants escaped and authorities of several states made a diligent effort to find them. They were in custody by June 30 and charged with first degree murder. They were tried, found guilty and sentenced to life in prison.

Fountain City has gained national recognition because of the historic Coffin House. Each year a festival called Levi Coffin Days is held in September. Although not sponsored for the benefit of the Coffin House, it raises funds for local activities. The festival draws a huge attendance and many Wayne County residents participate in the activities.

Economy, Main Street looking west, 1908. Courtesy of Jack Phelps

Chapter 11

Perry Township

Settlers came into what is now Perry Township in 1813. After Indiana had become a state in 1816, Perry Township was one of the first six to be formed. Land was taken from Perry to form Dalton, Jefferson, Green and Clay, bringing it down to one of the smaller townships in the county.

As in several other townships in Wayne County, Perry's first settlers were Quakers. Many came from Tennessee and for a time Economy was known as the Tennessee settlement. Other settlers moved into the area and according to one historian, the community appeared to have two distinct cultures which prevailed. Quakers were straight-laced and frowned on outward show. Outside of town the easterners and old country descendants were not so reserved in their conduct.

Economy is the only town in Perry Township and it was recorded in 1825. It was laid out by Charles Osborn who stated it would be "economy to build the town over on the hill." His statement was in regard to its residents being in less danger of malaria or swamp fever, known as "chills and aiggy" (ague). This disease caused the death of many people living near swamps and dense forest lowlands.

Economy was a trading center for a radius of about five miles. This was the distance a horse could travel in two hours on poor roads. Education was an important concern to the Quakers who built a Friends School for their own children in Economy. After 1857 other children could attend one of the four township schools located in the four corners of the township. In 1867 a brick four-room school was built at the edge of town which included the children of the Friends School. The country schools were closed and in 1907 a twelve year school was built. The

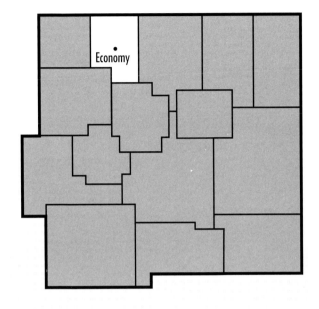

Year formed: 1817

Town: Economy

1990 Township Population: 700

Size: 18 Square Miles

Waterways: Morgan's Creek, Martindale Creek

Topography: Rolling and hilly, very little flat land.

Main roads: U.S. 35, Sugar Grove Road

A Pictorial History of Wayne County, Indiana

J. Seward Beard's Hardware Store, Economy, circa 1900. He refused to sell any tobacco products in his store for human consumption. Courtesy of Lewis Farmer

Family reunion at Osborn Lake, Economy. circa 1895–1900. It was a popular place for excursion trains coming from Richmond. Courtesy of Lewis Farmer

W. E. Oler Stockyards, east of Economy elevator. W. E. Oler at left is standing by the pens. They are loading the first car of hogs at Economy in 1901. Courtesy of Lewis Farmer

last graduating class from the Economy was in 1962 when Perry Township became part of the Nettle Creek School Corporation. It served as an elementary school until it was closed in 1971.

The CR&M railroad came through Economy in 1901 and was seen as a great improvement. Many men and boys earned money from working with the contractors. A horse team could earn $3.00 a day for their owners. Nearby farms boarded some of the workmen and several town women housed and fed the men who built the water tank and the depot. As soon as the line was finished to Richmond, W. E. Oler, a well known stock buyer, shipped eighty-two hogs in his first load from Economy. They averaged two hundred nine pounds each and farmers were paid $5.60 per hundred weight.

Economy, Main Street looking east showing the Central Hotel on the left, 1908. Courtesy of Lewis Farmer

A Pictorial History of Wayne County, Indiana

Horse drawn school hack, circa 1911. Children are carrying their books and dinner buckets. Collection of Carolyn Lafever

Lee Lamb, rural mail carrier on his last route, in front of the Economy Post Office, 1914. Courtesy of Priscilla Haisley

Jungle Doctor, Herbert C. Clark of Economy at seventy-five years of age. He was director of Gorgas Memorial Lab in Panama and spent over forty years in the study of tropical disease. The picture is from an article in the Saturday Evening Post, Oct. 4, 1952. Courtesy of Priscilla Haisley

Tom Stuart and Charlie Mendenhall standing in front of the Economy Elevator, circa 1920s. Mendenhall owned the elevator from 1921 to 1935, when it was sold to Harold Tharp. Courtesy of Lewis Farmer

Farmers, business men and travelers were quick to take advantage of the new transportation. Instead of an occasional trip on the long hard road to Richmond, one could get on the train, arrive in a short time and have the whole day to spend. In later years school sports teams rode the train to nearby towns for their games. A grain elevator was built at Economy shortly after the railroad was finished. The creamery was started in 1902 and the telephone was brought to town in 1903 by way of the Modoc Telephone Company in Randolph County. Economy had a hotel which prospered until it burned in 1912. In 1919 electricity became available in town.

Five generations have lived on the Cain farm, now the Maple Shade farms. The farm home is at the corner of Macy and Newman roads, a short distance from U.S. 35 and the railroad. Zora Cain was quick to capitalize on the nearness of the railroad. She encouraged her children to sell garden produce to the people on the

Economy School, home of the Economy Cardinals, was built in 1907 as a twelve-year school. It became part of the Nettle Creek School Corporation in 1962. The building remained as a grade school until 1971, when it was closed. Collection of Carolyn Lafever

Perry Township Volunteer Fire Department truck in the Economy 1974 parade. A. Cassiello stands on the running board. Courtesy of Lewis Farmer

Pine Hill Bison Farm, 1997, located on Robinson Road, is a bison breeding farm. Bison, or buffalo, are raised as a low-fat meat source. Photo by Ed Lafever

Six-horse hitch and one in training, owned by Amish farmer, Eli Lapp, 1997. The Belgian horses are pulling a disk and clod breaker. Photo by Ed Lafever

Maple Shade Farm, 1956, owned by Forest and J. B. Cain. The house faces the railroad and U.S. 35. and in front of it was the highest point on the C&O Railroad. Trains stopped sometimes to buy farm produce. The farm has been in the family since 1892. Courtesy of Maple Shade Farms

train as it passed their house. In later years Mrs. Cain was confined to a wheel chair and spent much of her time on the porch. Every day she waved to the train as it went by. At her death in July, 1966 a large wreath was placed on the door where the train crew could see it. A couple of days later the train came by, stopped for a few minutes and blew the whistle to honor the passing of their friend.

A remarkable family named Clark came to Economy in 1860. William Clark had made considerable money in North Carolina but saw war coming and did everything he could to get away. He loaned money to pork traders in Indiana and in 1858 he sent two of his older sons to the North. Elwood Clark took charge of a drygoods store in Economy and Jonathan went to

Philadelphia to study medicine. Son Addison later attended Earlham College and was one of its first graduates. The Clark family was noted for its talents and for the number of descendants who took up the medical profession.

One of the most famous of the Clark doctors was known as the "Jungle Doctor." Dr. Herbert C. Clark, once of Economy, went to Panama when General Gorgas asked for a young pathologist who would come down for six months until a regular man could be found. The canal was being built and disease was rampant. The six months stretched into years of study on tropical diseases. In 1929 Dr. Clark became director of the Gorgas Memorial Laboratory in Panama. He died in 1960 and his grave is in the Economy Cemetery.

Lois Beard, 1902–1979, compiled a history called "The Economy Times" in 1975. At that time there was a bank, the elevator, several small stores and service stations and the Economy Tile Company. They have all closed except one store and the tile works. The Lions Club and the Fire Department promote community activities. The present churches include the Economy Methodist and the Ministries of the Lamb. Perry Township has several Amish residents who came from Pennsylvania in the 1990s.

William and Susanna Smith acquired their farm in Webster Township in 1873. Family members lived in the house until 1994 when it was sold. The farm is still owned by great granddaughter Marcia Jeffers and her husband, Malcolm. Courtesy of Marcia Jeffers

Webster Township

The smallest township in Wayne County was also the last to be formed. On December 5, 1870, one hundred twenty-eight people who lived in the adjacent corners of Center, Wayne, New Garden and Green townships asked for their own township to be formed. It would surround the village of Dover (Webster). The village was platted in 1850 and in 1870 there were two churches, several business places, a post office and children could attend school at the Friends Academy. The county commissioners granted the petition and the new township was called Webster.

As soon as the township was formed there was a move to have the Friends school become a public school. In 1872 the brick school house was given over to the township and used for eleven years. A new-graded school building was opened in 1883 and the old school torn down. This was the first school built by Webster Township.

The name of Dover, named for the Dover meeting of Friends, stopped being used about 1871 when the Webster I.O.O.F. lodge was established. Webster had been the name of the post office since it began in 1851. Webster is the only town in the township although there is a residential and business area at the intersection of U.S. 35 and Indiana 38 called Silver Point. The highways were built after the 1930s, but there has been a road intersection at that place from the county's earliest days. Silver Point is not a village or town, but has had business places for many years.

The building of a railroad to Webster Township was proposed in 1900. The Cincinnati, Richmond and Muncie railroad wanted to come through the town and asked for a subsidy of $6,000. The issue was voted down so the railroad purchased a right of way at the west edge of the village and refused to let trains make stops there. The

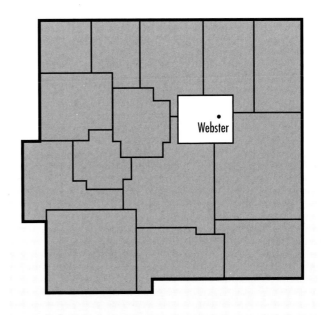

Year formed: 1870

Town: Webster, unincorporated

1990 Township Population: 1,321

Size: 15 Square Miles

Waterways: Noland's Fork

Topography: Gently rolling and erosion prone

Main roads: U.S. 35, Indiana 38

A Pictorial History of Wayne County, Indiana

Webster United Methodist. Built in 1865, it was originally called the Dover M.E. Church and the village of Webster was called Dover until 1871. Photo by Carolyn Lafever

Webster School, built in 1910, added a gymnasium in 1950. In 1962, Webster Township became part of Northeastern School Corporation. The bars in front of the school were to keep cars from driving up the sidewalk. Courtesy of Marcia Jeffers

Bank barn and windmill, 1918, owned by Marcia Jeffers' family for the past one hundred twenty-four years. Bank barns were built so that two stories had easy access. Courtesy of Marcia Jeffers

maneuver worked and the village people saw their mistake. They compromised with the railroad and the townspeople raised $1,000 for a depot and gave the company room for switches. The first train stop was in 1901 and for many years there was passenger and mail service by the railroad.

Webster had two churches, a Friends and a Methodist. The Friends church disbanded and was taken over by the First Baptist. The large cemetery still remains, but the building has been sold and is a private home. The Webster United Methodist Church was organized in 1865 as the Dover M.E. Church and the building was built a few months later. This is the only church in town. One of its special ministries is a men's breakfast every other Saturday morning. Men from the community meet for prayer and fellowship.

Jerry Fisher stands in front of Bob's Corner Cupboard in Webster. Owned by Bob Plankenhorn, this was a local meeting place for the "Class of '48." Picture is from the school yearbook of 1948. Courtesy of Marcia Jeffers

A Pictorial History of Wayne County, Indiana

Square Dancers from Webster High School, 1953–1954. They appeared on television in Cincinnati and Muncie. Left to Right: Dalton Dalzell, teacher, Charles Bond, Linda Smith, Joseph L. Tutterow, Nancy Culy, Mr. Richter, Judy Fields, John Reimer, Joan Crome, Richard Wickett, Eli Jackson, caller. Courtesy of Aileen Wickett

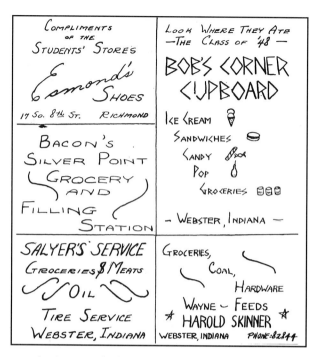

Several Webster Township business places put advertisements in the 1948 Webster High School yearbook. Courtesy of Marcia Jeffers

Young James Tutterow sits on the front of Webster's 1976 Bicentennial float. The float was in the Richmond Rose Parade, the Fountain City and Webster parades. Courtesy of Aileen Wicket

Webster General Store and Post Office, 1997. The post office was in the store until the 1970s when it was upgraded to third-class. The building was divided and the post office has its own room. It is the oldest post office in its original building in Wayne County. Photo by Carolyn Lefever

Webster Township Volunteer Fire Department, 1997. The Webster school was demolished except for the gymnasium which was remodeled for the fire department in 1969. Photo by Carolyn Lafever

Richmond Seventh-Day Adventist School on U.S. 35. This small school is an example of the many private schools in Wayne County. Photo by Carolyn Lafever

Rod Gilmore celebrating his twenty-first birthday with the community, Feb. 1988. Rod was afflicted with muscular dystrophy. The Rod Gilmore Foundation was organized by Webster Township people to help him and others with similar needs. Courtesy of Aileen Wickett

The Hillcrest Baptist Church is located at Silver Point. The church was organized in 1964 and the church built in 1972. For a few years the church operated The Hillcrest Christian School but it has been closed. Another very small private school in Webster Township is the Richmond Seventh-Day Adventist School.

Webster Township provided well for the education of the children. The last school was built in 1910 and had all twelve grades. In 1950 a gymnasium was added. The school reorganization of 1962 brought Webster into the Northeastern School Corporation. The older children went to Williamsburg and the school closed in 1967. The first building was razed in 1970 and the gymnasium was kept for the Webster Fire Department. Webster's basketball team was called the Pirates.

The community of Webster lost much of its vitality when the school closed. A once strong business community has been reduced to one general store and the post office. Other business places are scattered throughout the township. Organizations which have remained active are the Activities Club, Webster Homemakers Club, the Fire Department and its auxiliary. These groups support and raise money for the needs of the community.

When first grader, Rod Gilmore was diagnosed with muscular dystrophy, the community rallied behind him and the Rodney Gilmore Foundation was started. Representatives of every organization and of business served on its board. They raised funds for Rod and for three other boys with similar needs. Rod Gilmore passed away in 1992. The Foundation disbanded in 1996.

There is still a love of community and a desire to support good things in Webster. The ladies come together for a style show and salad bar once a year. But as older people pass on and younger ones do not feel the same community ties, it becomes harder. Each new generation has the responsibility of finding ways to hold on to community spirit and to learn to love their neighbors.

Lake Erie Depot in Milton, circa 1910. Located across the street from the Methodist church, it was torn down in the 1940s. Courtesy of Mary C. Sample

Chapter 12

Washington Township

Washington Township is considered to have some of the best agricultural lands in the state. Much of it is in the valley formed by the Whitewater, Greens Fork and Nolan's Fork of the Whitewater River. Because of the many waterways and the long drop of elevation through Wayne County, this area has been prone to flooding. From the 1930s to 1960s the Agricultural Stabilization Program of the Federal Government paid for a soil conservation effort by putting small dams all over the county. This helps to slow the flow of the rivers and streams. Washington was one of the first six townships and is the third largest in the county. Its only town is Milton, located on the west fork of the Whitewater river. Milton is the community center for the township.

Prior to 1837 the old National Road came through Milton, which was one of the main stops along the road. The town was platted in 1824 and by 1826 its population reached two hundred. It was a prominent point on the mail route from Columbus, Ohio to Indianapolis. The original old National Road came through Milton, but in the later survey the swamps in Hancock County caused it to be moved one mile north. Milton's first name was Milltown for the several mills located in and near there.

Hopes for the town were renewed when the Whitewater Canal was built through Washington Township in 1842. It looked as if Milton would become the largest town in Wayne County. Hotels, warehouses, mills and boat yards were built. On January 1, 1847 a flood damaged the feeder dams and the aqueduct near Cambridge City. The costly repairs caused a decline of the canal's usefulness and it was out of business by the 1860s.

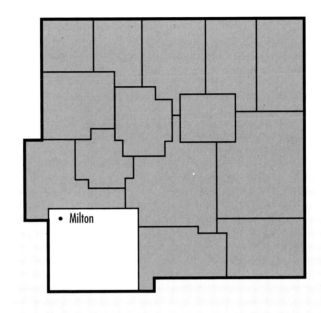

Year formed: 1817

Town: Milton

1990 Township Population: 1,539

Size: 42 Square Miles

Waterways: West Fork of the Whitewater River, Greens Fork River, Noland's Fork

Topography: East side is flat, west side hilly

Main roads: Indiana 1

A Pictorial History of Wayne County, Indiana

Beeson-Druley Homestead Farm on Indiana 1, south of Milton. Benjamin and Dorcas Beeson purchased the land in 1814. It has remained in the family, owned today by Pauline and Ivan Druley. Photo by Carolyn Lafever

Milton iron bridge, spanning the Whitewater River. Photo taken from a stereoscope card dated 1881. The lower part of the sign reads, "$500 fine for driving or riding faster than a walk over this bridge." The bridge was used for over one hundred years. Courtesy of Richard Huddleston

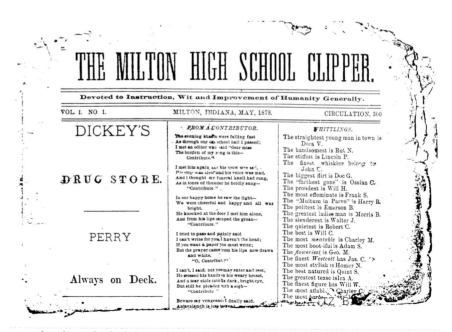

The Milton High School Clipper. The first edition of the Milton High School newspaper in 1878. The first class to graduate in 1879 had two students. Courtesy of Cambridge City Library

Milton, Central Avenue, circa 1900. Gas lights are on the street corners. Courtesy of Mary C. Sample

Fortunately for Milton the canal tow path was purchased by the Whitewater Valley Railroad and all was not lost. By the turn of the century there were two railroads operating through Milton and it was a prosperous town. Washington Township built its first public school in 1866, although there had been schools in the township as early as 1811. Milton was progressive in education and the new school used the graded system, meaning classes were separated according to the school year. First grade in one room, second grade in another, etc. The first graduating class was in 1879 with two students. The present school building was built behind the old one in 1924. Washington Township consolidated with the Western Wayne Schools in 1962 and the last class graduated from Milton in 1963. The building was used as an elementary school until 1995 when all the children were sent to the schools in Cambridge City.

In 1904 Milton had another cause for excitement. George Calloway, a Milton resident, was a member of a group from Indianapolis who gave permission for the interurban company to build a line from Indianapolis to Richmond. He refused to sign unless the company would build a two-mile branch line to Milton from Cambridge City. The company agreed and Calloway signed. The little electric car called the "Dinky" traveled from Milton to Cambridge City every hour from six in the morning until eleven at night. The Dinky stopped running in 1925 when automobiles became cheaper and roads improved.

Over the years Milton was home to several manufacturing enterprises. John Wisler was a famous maker of coverlets and was one of the townships early settlers. The Hoosier Drill Works started in 1859 and moved to Richmond in 1877. Other manufacturers were Doddridge-Beck casket company and Helm Manufacturing company which made safes for home use.

One of the surprises of Washington Township graces a hill on Sarver Road near Milton. In 1865 Isaac Kinsey built a magnificent home in the Italianate architectural style and called it "Beechwood." Kinsey, a Wayne County industrialist and merchant, had helped finance a successful strike by his brothers in the California

Ora White's store in Milton, circa 1920. White is standing beside the Red Crown Gasoline pump. The sign reads "gasoline 28 (cents)," the 30 has been crossed out. The store burned in 1923. Courtesy of Betty Williamson

Advertisement in the Clevenger's directory of farmers in Wayne County, 1919. Farms advertised like other business for many years. Courtesy of Ethel Sieweke

The Cambridge City/Milton interurban line or "Dinky" began service in 1904 and closed in 1925. It was a spur line from Cambridge City connecting with the line from Richmond to Terre Haute. The two-mile trip was made several times a day. Courtesy of Mary C. Sample

Maude Belle Templin's Bakery and Restaurant, circa 1924, on the Main Street of Milton. Mrs Templin stands in the doorway. The building was demolished in 1932. Courtesy of Mary C. Sample

gold rush. The house was honored in 1975 as one of Indiana's finest Victorian country homes. It was selected to be recorded as a Historic American Building by the Office of Archaeology and Historic Preservation of Washington, D.C.

Manlove Park was located about one mile north of Milton on Indiana 1. It was founded in 1866 by Joseph Manlove. The park once had a 22-room hotel and facilities for boating, tennis and croquet. The lake in the park was eight feet deep and about three-quarters of a mile long. It boasted a unique water lilies display which brought visitors from as far away as Cincinnati. For about thirty years it was one of the most popular recreation parks in the county. It closed in 1916 when the lake began going dry. The ornate arched entrance was moved to another park. The present day gravel pit of Irving Materials Inc. has taken over what was once the lake.

In 1950 an outdoor concrete skating ring was built by the Boost Milton Club. About the same time free movies were shown on warm summer evenings on the side of one of the business buildings. People brought their chairs and sat across the street to view the show. Free movies were sponsored by the merchants, usually the grocery stores, to encourage more shopping in town.

Interesting people from Washington Township include Jack and Patricia Bohlander who for thirty-one years have operated Poor Jack Amusements, Indiana's largest carnival. Jack passed away in 1997. Also notable are Albert Ferris, farmer and state legislator, his son Merrill and his daughter-in-law, Mary. Merrill was serving on the Board of Directors for the Indiana Farm Bureau from District VI when he was struck down with leukemia in 1986. Mary, his wife, was chosen to succeed him on the Board

A Pictorial History of Wayne County, Indiana

Glenn W. Sample graduating from Purdue, 1935. Originally from Milton, Sample worked for thirty years with the Farm Bureau and was editor of the *Hoosier Farmer*. His work on behalf of Ivy Tech State College was honored by giving his name to the North Meridian Center in Indianapolis. Courtesy of Mary C. Sample

Milton Methodist Church built in 1875. The pointed steeple was struck by lightning and it was replaced with a bell tower. Courtesy of Mary C. Sample

H. D. Huddleston Plumbing next to Templin's Bakery and Restaurant in Milton, circa 1920. Huddleston moved his business to Cambridge city in 1933. Courtesy of the Cambridge City Library

Milton school building, 1972. Built in 1924, the last class graduated in 1963. It was consolidated with Western Wayne School Corporation and was used as an elementary school until 1995. Courtesy of Mary C. Sample

Milton's postal station. It was given to the Wayne County Museum in 1962, when the post office was remodeled. This type of compact station was often used in general stores. Photo by Carolyn Lafever

Valley Grove Cemetery Memorial Stone at Milton. A small non-denominational chapel was built on this site in 1889 to provide accommodations for funerals. It was taken down, a large hole dug, and the church buried on the site in 1990. Photo by Carolyn Lafever

Pauline Druley, the first women secretary of the Indiana Senate, 1961–1963. Her family was among first settlers in Washington Township. She graduated in 1931 from Earlham College and resides in Milton with her husband of sixty years, Ivan Druley. Courtesy of Pauline Druley

becoming the first woman to hold this position. In 1992 Morris Jobe received the Sagamore of the Wabash award for service to his community and for fifteen years of state service.

Washington Township is still a strong farming community. Milton town's business has declined since the Washington Township bank merged with People's State Bank and moved to Cambridge City in 1932. Other losses were the closing of Dodderidge-Beck casket company in 1963 and moving the high school to Cambridge City in 1963. Although the school building remained a grade school for several more years, the rallying cheers for the Milton Sharpshooters basketball team were no more. Community activities today are sponsored by the Milton Methodist and the Milton Christian churches, the clubs and organizations.

Main Street, Richmond, 1931, looking west. The explosion in 1968 occurred at the corner of 6th and Main, right side of picture. The Marting Arms store, source of the explosion, was on the south side corner of Main across 6th from Vigran's. The buildings across Main Street from the explosion were badly damaged. Courtesy of Wayne County Museum

Chapter 13

Wayne Township

History accords two Kentucky adventurers, Richard Rue and George Holman as being the first white people to enter and settle the area known as Wayne County. In 1805 they, with other family members, took possession of their sections lying between Short Creek and Elkhorn Creek, south of Richmond. Their land was in what became Wayne Township. The next to settle in the township were David Hoover and his companions, Quakers or Friends from North Carolina. They discovered the many natural advantages of the area including the pure spring water coming from the banks of streams. They found good limestone, rich soil and an abundant water supply which would make suitable places for mills.

In a short time other settlers came, primarily Friends from southern states. John Smith owned much of the land east of the Whitewater River and south of what is Richmond's Main Street. Almost from the beginning this became known as "Smithville." In 1816 Smith hired David Hoover to divide some of his land into lots. The population of the settlement was about one hundred fifty. In 1818 the name was changed to Richmond and the town was incorporated. From 1820 to 1827, when talk of canals began, there was a rush of land speculators, city builders and settlers coming to the area. In 1828 the survey for the National Road placed it on the village's main street and the anticipation of road and canal construction gave Richmond a big boost. By 1840 Richmond's population had grown to 2,070 and it was chartered a city.

Mills were about the first commercial ventures in the county. The last remaining mill site which still has early mill buildings is in Middleboro. It was the sixth mill built in Wayne County, first constructed in 1826 by Jeremiah

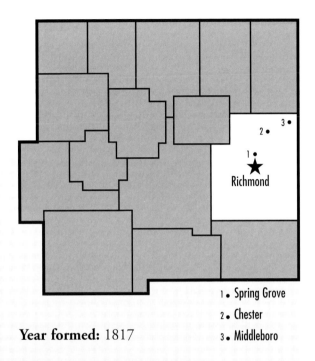

1 • Spring Grove
2 • Chester
3 • Middleboro

Year formed: 1817

Town: Richmond, Spring Grove Middleboro, Chester

1990 Township Population: 44,743

Size: 53 square miles

Waterways: Whitewater River and its three branches, East Fork, Middle Fork and West Fork; Elkhorn and Short Creek

Topography: Mostly rolling with Whitewater River Gorge through the center

Main roads: Interstate 70, U.S. 40, U.S. 35, Indiana 27, Indiana 227

A Pictorial History of Wayne County, Indiana

Site of Cox's Mill in Middleboro, the sixth mill built in Wayne County. The brick structure was built in 1860 to replace the stone mill on the same property, built in 1826 by Jeremiah Cox. The last mill building has been used as a residence for many years. Photo by Ed Lafever

The Methodist Episcopal Church, Chester. It relocated from the town to U.S. 27 and is called the Chester Heights United Methodist Church. It was organized when the local Friends church refused to allow the burial of a local Civil War soldier in its cemetery because of Quaker opposition to the war. Courtesy of the Wayne County Museum

The village of Chester in 1913. U.S. 27 made a sharp turn as it went through the town. The "dog-legged corner" was the scene of many accidents. It was straightened in 1958 and the highway misses the town completely. Courtesy of Foster Gallery

Dr. W. W. Zimmerman, his wife Cyrena and daughter Lona. He served as Richmond's mayor for three terms, 1898–1905, 1910–1913, 1918–1922. During his terms as mayor, he was still able to continue his medical practice. Courtesy of Jim Stevenson

Cox II. His father, Jeremiah Cox, was one of the first two men to lay out lots in Richmond. The old stone building at the back of the Middleboro site was used until 1860 when a new mill was built at the side of the road. A small settlement grew up around the area first known as Cox's Mill, then as Middleboro.

The National Road, the most important east-west highway of the pioneer period brought increased amounts of traffic and commerce to Wayne County. A railroad was built to Richmond and the first steam locomotive arrived in 1853. The Industrial Revolution which started in England had begun to take hold in the United States before the Civil War. After the war ended in 1865, there was another period of industrial change from primarily agricultural to manufacturing enterprises. It was in areas like Richmond where these changes took place.

Although there were many Quaker settlers in Wayne Township, there were German crafts-men and Italian railroad workers who made their

Chester in 1997. Horsin Around is one of the few businesses left in town. Photo by Ed Lafever

A Pictorial History of Wayne County, Indiana

Main Street Bridge, Richmond, Ind.

The second bridge over the Whitewater River and the gorge in Richmond. The steel bridge replaced the old wooden covered bridge in 1897. The weight of interurban cars so weakened the bridge that it was closed in 1915. The current bridge is due for replacement. Courtesy of Larry Fansher

The old city building in Richmond, 1900. It was built in 1886 and used until a new building was completed in 1968 on Main and North 5th. Courtesy of Jim Stevenson

A Sunday School parade in August 1908 on Main Street, Richmond. The Union Mission was organized by the Women's Christian Temperance Union in 1898 and was supported by several of the local churches. One of its programs was a night school to help Hungarians perfect their English and writing. Courtesy of Wayne County Museum

Mr. and Mrs. Andrew Walker sitting on the running board of their huckster wagon, a truck fitted with shelves to carry grocery items to rural areas. Walker operated a grocery store at 1112 South M. Street from 1907–1943. Upon retirement he rebuilt the store into an apartment house. Courtesy of Foster Gallery

home in Richmond. In the census of 1900, about 30 percent of Richmond's residents claimed German ancestry. Wayne County was also one of the main routes for black slaves on the Underground Railroad before and during the Civil War. The county, and particularly Richmond and Fountain City, became home to this growing minority population.

Manufacturing plants of one type or another brought prosperity early to Richmond. Mills and other industries requiring mechanical power were located near the Whitewater River. When steam power came into general use the factories started to locate close to the railroad near North E. Street. By 1910 Richmond had one hundred twenty-five factories and was a leader in the manufacture of threshing machines, traction engines and balers, lawn mowers, roller skates, grain drills, burial caskets, ventilating devices for green houses, and fire fighting helmets. Improved agricultural implements were manufactured by Gaar, Scott & Co. 1849–1919 and Swayne, Robinson & Co. 1841–1997. Wayne Agricultural Co. launched in Dublin, 1837, eventually became Wayne Works of Richmond, manufacturers of school buses until 1992. From 1901–1941, fourteen manufacturers

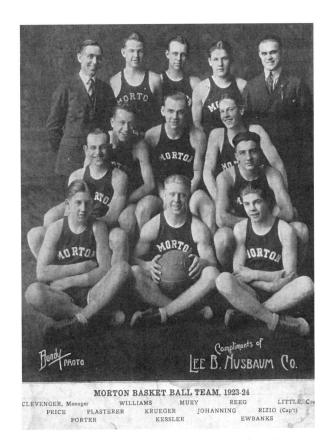

MORTON BASKET BALL TEAM, 1923-24

CLEVENGER, Manager   WILLIAMS   MUEY   REEG   LITTLE, Coa
PRICE   PLASTERER   KRUEGER   JOHANNING   RIZIO (Cap't)
PORTER   KESSLER   EWBANKS

Basketball Team of Morton High School, 1923–1924. Richmond's Morton school was built on North 9th Street in 1910. In 1940 the present Richmond High School on Hub Etchison Parkway opened its doors to students. Courtesy of Foster Gallery

A Pictorial History of Wayne County, Indiana

Gennett Recording Laboratory, Richmond, 1923. Art Landry with his "Call of the North Orchestra" making a record. In the 1920s Starr-Gennett Company was a broad-based musical empire, producing millions of records, in addition to pianos and phonographs. The depression of the 1930s put Gennett records out of business. Courtesy of Sam Meier

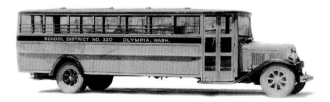

Wayne Bus, 1930s. In 1875 the Wayne Agricultural Co. moved to Richmond from Dublin. It manufactured farm implements, buggies, and carriages and in 1904 the company made the "Richmond" automobile. One of the first motor-powered school buses was made by Wayne Works in 1914. Courtesy of Foster Gallery

Templin's Grocery Store on south 9th Street, circa 1935. Grocery in business at the height of the depression of the 1930s. Left to right: Smitty, the clerk, Mrs. and Mr. Templin, owners. Courtesy of Mary C. Sample

built automobiles in Richmond. Other companies which built large plants in Richmond were NATCO, Belden Corp., Perfect Circle, and International Harvester. Hill's Roses brought international fame to Richmond for their production of cut roses.

Wayne Township has other small towns although Richmond covers much of the township. Chester is located about four miles north of Richmond and U.S. 27 once passed through it. The State Highway Commission straightened the road in 1958, taking out the dangerous corner turn through the village.

For a time Chester had quite a bit of commerce. It was named by Joshua Jeffers an early settler from Chester County, Pennsylvania. It had a tavern, a country store, post office and a small newspaper called "The Chester Gazette." Some residents felt that both World War II and moving the road caused major changes for the town. Farmers around Chester began working in

Painting in the park. Richmond Art Club, Kenneth Gregg's class, circa 1940s. Gregg was an artist and taught in the Richmond Community School System. Courtesy of Foster Gallery

A Pictorial History of Wayne County, Indiana

Richmond High School built in 1940. It was the first high school in the nation to have an orchestra, and the only one known to have an art gallery on its campus. Drawing by Jack Phelps

Springwood Lake, Richmond. For many years this was a popular recreation park for fishing, swimming and boating. It is now called Springwood Lake Park. Courtesy of Larry Fansher

Downtown Richmond, 1950s. The Hoosier Store is on the left and directly across the street was the Marting Arms, source of the explosion in 1968. Two explosions and fire destroyed all the buildings along the south side of the street and badly damaged others on both sides of the street. Courtesy of Foster Gallery

Specialty Record Shop, 534 Main Street. Owners Henry Bass (left), Ina Rile Bass, Elizabeth Rile Kelley and Harold Kelley operated the business from 1946–1980. After the explosion damaged the store, it was rebuilt and was the first store to be back in business. Courtesy of Harold Kelley

Richmond factories during the war. When the road was changed, fewer people came to do business. Chester has never been incorporated.

Spring Grove is a town within a city, surrounded by Richmond. Many people who drive on Chester Blvd. do not realize they are passing through another town. It was incorporated in 1884, has no main street, grocery stores or restaurants. Its strict zoning rules allow only an area for professional offices, a nursing home and churches. The rest of the town is zoned for single family residences. Until 1968 Reid Memorial Hospital was in Spring Grove, but by mutual agreement Spring Grove gave the hospital to Richmond so federal funds could be received for expanding it. Most of the tax revenue is used for fire protection.

Things seemed to be going as usual for Richmond until one sunny Saturday April 6, 1968. At 1:47 in the afternoon in the heart of Richmond's downtown two explosions occurred, the second more powerful than the first. A huge black cloud of smoke rose from the blast and soon a huge fire was burning buildings close by. The explosions came from the Marting Arms, a sporting goods store at the southeast corner of Sixth

Explosion in Richmond, April 6, 1968. Seventeen minutes after the first explosion huge clouds of black smoke poured from the fire on Main Street. The photographer was facing east between 4th and 5th Streets. Courtesy of Jim Stevenson

Explosion shown from North 6th Street, within a half block of the fire. The Hoosier Store is on the left. It is now the 600 Building. Forty-one people lost their lives and more than one hundred were injured. Courtesy of Jim Stevenson

Spring Grove, Friends United Meeting and the Quaker Hill Bookstore. Photo by Ed Lafever

Richmond's Main Street Promenade, 1972. The pedestrian promenade was constructed after the devastating explosion of 1968. Several blocks of Main Street were closed to east-west traffic. It was awarded a National Landscaping Award in 1973, presented by the first lady Patricia Nixon in Washington. It was removed in 1997. Courtesy of James Brower

and Main. It was never determined what set off the first explosion, but the second came from igniting gunpowder stored in the basement of Marting Arms.

Richmond's Fire Department, Civil Defense and all of the emergency services available were quick to join the effort. Other fire fighters and emergency help came from as far as one hundred fifty miles away to aid in the disaster. The toll from the explosion and fire was the deaths of forty-one men, women and children and more than one hundred injured. Eight buildings were leveled and damage was noted over a 14-square-block area.

Richmond moved forward after the tragedy to rebuild the downtown. Several buildings had to be torn down and new ones built. A new plan

for Main Street was developed with local funds and federal grants. Five blocks of the street were closed to east-west traffic and a pedestrian mall was built. Its design brought national recognition to the city. It lasted twenty-five years but did not fulfill the long-term expectations of its builders. The Promenade was removed and the street opened in 1997.

Richmond covers much of Wayne Township but there is quite a bit of rural property and farms, especially in the northeast corner. I-70 serves as a by-pass for the city. This has cut down traffic congestion which used to come through on U.S. 40. Each decade has brought change to Richmond, some for better, some not so good.

Spring Grove. A new medical building across the street from Reid Hospital. Spring Grove does not allow other types of commercial business within the corporation limits. Many of Richmond's medical offices and clinics are located in Spring Grove. Photo by Ed Lafever

Audrey, 74, and Mary Reichter, 72, in their home which has sheltered more than one thousand foster children for over fifty years. They were honored with "Distinguished Hoosier" awards from Gov. Frank O'Bannon in 1997. Courtesy of Audrey and Mary Reichter

The Scales of Justice by artists William and Jeanne Magaw for Richmond's Municipal City Building. The metal sculpture was commissioned for the 200th anniversary of the U.S. Constitution and dedicated September 21, 1987. The small figures on the scales represent the freedoms guaranteed by the Bill of Rights. Photo by Carolyn Lafever

In 1986–1987 Richmond was honored as an All-American City. In the early 1980s manufacturing was still doing well. But over the past ten years many factories have closed or moved away. Downtown business has declined, much of it moving nearer the I-70 exits. In the 1990s several revitalization efforts in urban renewal, historic preservation, business and economic development have brought in new business and tourism.

Richmond has a long history of culture and education. Earlham College was started by the Quakers in 1847 and continues as an outstanding educational institution. The Earlham School of Religion and the Bethany Seminary are located on the campus. Indiana University East and Ivy Tech are also respected institutions of higher education. Richmond has three outstanding libraries, Morrisson-Reeves, Earlham's Lilly Library and the IU East library.

The Wayne County Historical Museum, one of the nation's finest county museums, is one of several cultural facilities in the city. The Richmond Art Museum is the result of area artists who started the Richmond Art Association in 1898. The Indiana Football Hall of Fame is an outstanding sports museum. The Gaar House Museum, a splendid restored Victorian home of the Gaar family, is located north of the city. Hayes Regional Arboretum, a 355-acre environmental education facility, displays species of trees and shrubs which are only native to the area. Outstanding music and theater are offered by the Whitewater Opera Co. and the Civic Theater.

The religious heritage of Wayne Township is one of its strongest links to its history and to the future. Congregations of various religious persuasion have built houses of worship all over the city. They provide spiritual nurture plus supporting all types of charitable work. Social services are offered by the Salvation Army, Circle U Help Center, Genesis of the YWCA, Dunn Center and Green Acres Rehabilitation Center, among many others.

Richmond is still the gateway to Indiana and the mid-west. The city offers good business opportunities, shopping, excellent restaurants and many outstanding cultural opportunities for its residents and visitors.

Wayne County Commissioners 1997: John O. Catey, District 1; Max A. Smith, District 3, Marcia T. French, District 2. Photo by Chagares Photography

Chapter 14

Wayne County – Looks Forward

Visitors to Wayne County today view a very different place from that seen by the settlers who came in 1804–1805. Those hardy men and women would wonder at the neat cultivated farm fields, wrenched so long ago by their hard work from dense hardwood forests. The wide smooth ribbons of road through the county are a marked contrast to the narrow trails which the pioneers followed. The crowded city with lights reflected for miles would astonish the settlers. They were used to dark nights with light coming only from the heavens. The face of Wayne County has changed in many ways since it belonged to Native Americans and to the creatures of the wild.

The population of Wayne County today is 71,951 (1990 U.S. Census). 53.7 percent live in urban areas, 46.3 percent live in the country. In 1996 there were 1,800 farms in Wayne County with an average of 150 acres per farm. However, the owner of one farm often rents other farm fields, resulting in one farmer raising crops on a large number of acres. Farming runs from general to highly specialized grain, cattle, hog and dairy operations. Agriculture is still of major importance to the economy of the county and the taxes paid by farmers and landowners are substantial. Business, factories, utilities and non-profit groups are important as they provide jobs and services for the area.

The government of Wayne County is essentially the same as it has been from 1810 when the county was first formed. There are three County Commissioners who take care of county business. The commissioners have a seven-member County Council who helps oversee the distribution of funds. There are many other offices which handle the greatly increased details of county busi-

**WAYNE COUNTY
SCHOOL CORPORATIONS**
Consolidated 1962

Centerville-Abington
Centerville Township
Abington Township

Nettle Creek
Clay Township
Dalton Township
Harrison Township
Jefferson Township
Perry Township

Northeastern Wayne
Franklin Township
Green Township
New Garden Township
Webster Township

Richmond Community Schools
Boston Township
Wayne Township

Western Wayne
Jackson Township
Washington Township

A Pictorial History of Wayne County, Indiana

Jim and Helen Cope with students at the Cope Environmental Center, Centerville. The nature preserve containing over one hundred species of exotic conifer trees. Courtesy of Cope Environmental Center

Old National Road Welcome Center for the Wayne County Convention and Tourism Bureau, 1997. Photo by Edward Lafever

Dedication day at the Fountain City Wesleyan Church, 1996. Begun in New Port (Fountain City) in 1843, it has continued to flourish. The new church building is located on U.S. 27 south of Fountain City. Courtesy of the Fountain City Wesleyan Church

In the past two years merchants have spent their own money to refurbish the charming old buildings in Greens Fork. It has generated increased interest and business for the town, 1997. Photo by Edward Lafever

ness and law enforcement. Some of the offices were instituted from the earliest days such as the County Clerk, who works with tax records, and the Sheriff, who handles law enforcement. In 1812 the officers of the county were appointed but most now are elected offices.

No one can predict the future with any degree of accuracy, but there are trends which give us an indication of what to expect. Since the 1960s there has been renewed interest in nature conservation and in the preservation of old buildings and historic districts. The exterior of the Wayne County Courthouse was refurbished in 1993 to celebrate its 100th birthday. It is one of many structures in the county to be listed on the National Register of Historic Places.

In 1992 the Parks Foundation and the Cope Environmental Center was founded on Shoemaker Road near Centerville. It is a 100-acre nature preserve dedicated to the wise stewardship of habitats for plant life, wildlife and humankind. Other efforts toward preserving nature are the in town and city parks, the Whitewater Gorge project and Hayes Regional Arboretum. Unlike fifty years ago, many people do not have direct contact with the land. Wayne County plans to continue providing children with a good understanding of nature and the rural heritage which is so important to the health and balance of life.

Another trend which has developed in the past decade is the move to take over valuable farm land for housing. Many urban residents have moved to the small towns and into the country causing a boom in housing. Several Amish families have moved to Wayne County from Pennsylvania building homes and large barns. They have given a fresh look to several farms throughout the county. Their horse-drawn carriages are a reminder of simpler times and that they are people of the land.

A Pictorial History of Wayne County, Indiana

Western Wayne Elementary School, Cambridge City. The latest public school to be built in Wayne County, opened in 1996. Photo by Carolyn Lafever

Bethany Theological Seminary. The Church of the Brethren moved their headquarters and seminary from Illinois to Richmond. They are next to the Earlham School of Religion on the campus of Earlham College. Photo by Carolyn Lafever

New farm buildings built by Amish farmer Eli Lapp in Perry Township, 1995–1997. It is primarily a dairy operation of three hundred sixty acres. Photo by Edward Lafever

Education for the children has always been important to the residents of Wayne County. In the early 1800s it was provided close to home. By the late 1800s the townships were building their own schools. In the 1960s–1970s ten townships lost their elementary or high schools and today there are only five school corporation. But the face of education has changed in other ways. In 1994–1995 12,298 children in Wayne County were enrolled in public schools, 597 children enrolled in private schools and 69 were schooled at home. Of the 5,742 students in grades 7-12, 2.9 percent left school without graduating. Of the 711 high school graduates in 1993–1994, 52 percent went on to higher education. Indiana's schools rank about the same per cent as the national average in graduates from high school.

Renovation of the Richmond Square Mall, 1997. Mall space was added for stores, restaurants and an expanded pedestrian area. Lush green plants and benches welcome customers. Photo by Edward Lafever

A Pictorial History of Wayne County, Indiana

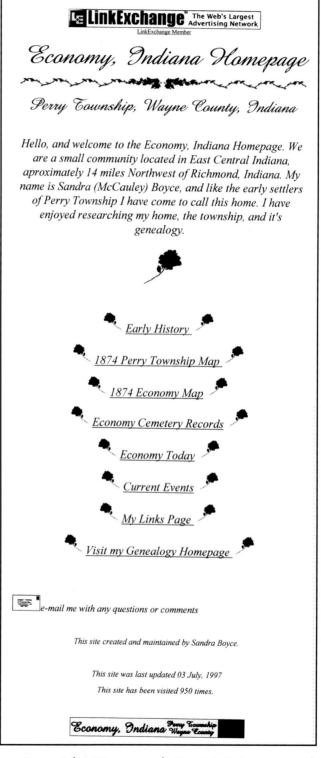

Economy, Indiana Homepage

Perry Township, Wayne County, Indiana

Hello, and welcome to the Economy, Indiana Homepage. We are a small community located in East Central Indiana, aproximately 14 miles Northwest of Richmond, Indiana. My name is Sandra (McCauley) Boyce, and like the early settlers of Perry Township I have come to call this home. I have enjoyed researching my home, the township, and it's genealogy.

Early History

1874 Perry Township Map

1874 Economy Map

Economy Cemetery Records

Economy Today

Current Events

My Links Page

Visit my Genealogy Homepage

e-mail me with any questions or comments

This site created and maintained by Sandra Boyce.

This site was last updated 03 July, 1997

This site has been visited 950 times.

Economy, Indiana Perry Township Wayne County

Economy, Indiana's Homepage on the Internet, 1997. Homepage created by Sandra Boyce

Wayne County Fairgrounds on Salisbury Road. In 1997 the Tom Raper Center was built to expand the facilities. Photo by Edward Lafever

One of Centerville's charming arches for which the old town is famous. Centerville has been known for its antique shops for many years and is part of "Indiana's Famous Antique Alley," along the U.S. 40, the Old National Road. Photo by Bob Blue

All over Wayne County plans are being made for the coming new century. In the works is an industrial park at Interstate 70 and Indiana 1 between Cambridge City and Hagerstown. Greens Fork has set an example for refurbishing business buildings on their small town main street. Richmond Square Mall spent months renovating and expanding. New industry is coming into the county, especially at the eastern edge of Richmond and many are optimistic about new opportunities.

A new source of community grants has come from the profits from the state lottery which has created a "Build Indiana" fund. Several non-profit organizations have been given grants for building or refurbishing projects. Local state legislators are continuing to help bring funds back to Wayne County.

The Richmond/Wayne County Convention and Tourism Bureau and the Richmond/Wayne County Chamber of Commerce promote the county for new business and tourism. Improvements are being made to attract new interest in Richmond such as Main Street of the downtown being opened up for automobile traffic. The five-block Promenade had been closed to east-west traffic from 1972–1997. The decline of the downtown spurred an effort to revitalize the area. In the next few years a much needed new bridge will be built over the Whitewater River. The bridge, to be built south of the old bridge, is part of U.S. 40 running through the city. Wayne County continues to maintain and improve its own roads, some of the best in the state.

Citizens of the county are coming to terms with new computer technology which has mushroomed since 1980. Computers have changed the way we do banking, receive messages, and educate ourselves. New technology continues to enable us to use our resources more efficiently. The challenge of the future is the same as the challenges of the past. We must learn to live with change while keeping the best of what we have learned from the past.

Museum Staff (left to right): James Waechter, Curator; Mary Maloney, Secretary; Michele Bottorff, Director. They stand under the picture of the Museum founder, Julia Meek Gaar

Wayne County Historical Museum, 1150 N. A Street, Richmond

The Scott House, N. 10th Street, Richmond. The Victorian Annex to the museum

Wayne County Historical Museum

The Old Settler's Association was the pioneer historical society of Wayne County. As early as 1859 early settlers were conducting an annual picnic and meeting in Centerville. In 1869 the association was formally organized. The old settlers related incidents from the county's early days, often showing household utensils, farm implements, clothing, furniture and other objects which related to pioneer life. From these annual events came the Wayne County Historical Association, formally organized in 1882.

The historical association flourished until about 1906. Items had been donated to them and the books, documents and pioneer items were kept in the Court House. Later they were stored on the third floor of the Morrisson-Reeves library. The historical society was reorganized as the Wayne County Historical Society in 1930, with Julia Meek Gaar as its president. She had traveled extensively and collected historical artifacts, including an Egyptian mummy, from all over the world. They were exhibited in a gallery in Richmond's Morton High School. Mrs. Gaar began negotiating with the Whitewater Monthly Meeting of Friends and acquired the old "Hicksites" meeting house in Richmond in 1930. The artifacts of the Historical Society and those of Mrs. Gaar were put together making an outstanding collection for the new museum.

The Wayne County Historical Museum is located on North A Street. The main collection is in the old meeting house and the grounds contain a Pioneer Village. The Scott House, a restored Victorian house, was given to the Museum in 1977 and is open to the public for tours and special events. The staff consists of a Director and a Curator and two part-time employees. Countless hours are given by volunteers for general help and as tour guides.

The Wayne County, Indiana, Historical Society is a non-profit, educational corporation. It receives a small annual grant from Wayne County, but depends upon donations, bequests, annual membership dues, admission and gift shop for its subsistence. The museum returns much to the county in preservation of historical artifacts and documents. Tours for the school children of Wayne County are free. The citizens of Wayne County are fortunate to have what is regarded by many as one of the outstanding local museums of the country.

BOOKS

Built Of Men, The Story of Indiana Cooperatives by I. Harvey Hull; Indiana Cooperatives; Harper Brothers, Publishers, New York 1952.

Cambridge City, 1836-1936, Cambridge City Centennial Committee.

Cambridge City, Indiana 1836-1961, One Hundred and Twenty-five Years, Cambridge City Chamber of Commerce.

A Century of Indiana by Edward E. Moore, American Book Company, New York, 1910.

Clevenger's Directory of Farmers and Breeders, Wayne County, Indiana. H. O. Clevenger, Mgr. Indianapolis, Indiana 1919.

Dublin, 1830-1980, Dublin, Indiana. Sesquicentennial Committee.

Economy Times by Lois Beard Lennox, Prepared for Economy, Indiana Sesquicentennial 1975.

Electric Railroads of Indiana by Jerry Marlette; Council for Local History, Indianapolis, 1959.

History of Centerville by Walter E. Spahr, Wayne County Historical Society 1966.

History of Indiana, Volume I. L. Esarey, The Hoosier Press, Fort Wayne, Indiana, 1924.

History of Northeastern Wayne County; Bicentennial Commision of "Old Newport Area," Unigraphics Inc., Evansville, Indiana, 1976.

History of Wayne County, Indiana Vol 1 & 2; Inter-State Publishing Co., Chicago, Illinois 1884.

History of Wayne County by Andrew W. Young; Robert Clarke & Co. , Cincinnati, Ohio, 1872.

Indiana Gazeteer, 1849-50.

Bibliography

Indiana in Transition, The Emergence of an Industrial Commonwealth, 1820–1920, by Clifton J. Phillips, Indiana Historical Bureau & Indiana Historical Society, Indianapolis, Indiana, 1968.

The Indiana Water Resource, 1980, Edited by G. Douglas Clark.

Memoirs of Wayne County and the City of Richmond, Indiana, Vol. 1 & 2 by Henry Clay Fox, Editor-In-Chief; Western Historical Association, Madison, Wisconsin, 1912.

Pioneer Sketches of the Upper White Water Valley by Bernard Knollenberg. Indiana Historical Society, Indianapolis, Indiana 1945.

Richmond, Eastern Gateway to Indiana by Daisy Marvel Jones, Richmond City Schools, Richmond, Indiana 1959.

The Rivers of Indiana, by Richard Simmons.

A Sesquicentennial History of Fountain City, Indiana 1984 by Jerrel Brooks and Gary Cole, Prinit Press, Dublin, Indiana.

Some Recollections Of My Boyhood by Branson L. Harris, 1908.

Travel Accounts of Indiana 1679–1961 Compiled by Shirley S. McCord, Indiana Historical Bureau, Indianapolis, Indiana. 1970.

Wheels Across America by Clarence P. Hornung. A.S. Barnes and Company, New York 1959.

MAP SOURCES

Atlas of Wayne County, Indiana, D. J. Lake; Griffing, Stevenson & Co. Philadelphia, Pennsylvania, 1874; Reprint 1974 by the Bookmark, Knightstown, Indiana.

Architectural and Historical Guide to Western Wayne, 1977.

Historic Sites of Wayne County, Indiana by Gertrude Ward, Wayne County Resource Inventory Council 1997.

Plat Book of Wayne County, Indiana 1994, 1997.

The County of Wayne, Indiana, Atlas and Art Folio, Rerick Brothers, Richmond, Indiana. 1893.

MAGAZINES AND NEWSPAPERS

Hagerstown Exponent Newspaper, Hagerstown, Indiana.

Cambridge City Tribune, Cambridge City, Indiana.

The Richmond Item, Richmond, Indiana.

The Palladium-Item, Richmond, Indiana.

MANUSCRIPTS

Aviation in Richmond, Indiana, 1909–1945 by Eugene E. Stegal, 1968.

Early History of New Garden Township, Wayne County, Indiana by Idris E. Hinshaw 1948.

History of Boston Township by Lewis M. Starr.

The History of Transportation in Wayne County, Indiana Part 1–6, by Luther M. Feeger, The Palladium-Item, Richmond, Indiana. March 1953-July 1954.

The Mills of Wayne County by William O. Wissler. Thesis for Earlham College June 19, 1912.

Minutes of the Old Settlers' Picnic, 1859–1929; Wayne County Historical Museum.

Index

Carolyn Lafever

Photo by Jim Stevenson

Carolyn Ruth Lafever has been writing about the history of Wayne County since Hagerstown celebrated its Sesquicentennial in 1982. Her project was a booklet for the community quilt which depicted history through the needlework of local women. The project led to an invitation to become a member of the Board of Trustees for Historic Hagerstown Museum. She served in several positions before becoming its first Director/Curator.

In 1992 she produced a video, *The Murals of Charles Newcomb*, for Historic Hagerstown. It was supported by an Indiana Heritage Research Grant, a joint effort of the Indiana Historical Society and the Indiana Humanities Council. From the research for the video, a book, *The Murals of Charles Newcomb*, was published in 1993. Both projects tell the story of murals painted on the walls and ceiling of the Odd Fellows Lodge's Public Hall on Main Street (now the Nettle Creek Valley Museum). They were painted in 1913 by local artist, Charles Newcomb, who took his subject from the work of Maxfield Parrish. The video and the book cover Hagerstown's early history.

The latest book produced by Mrs. Lafever is *The Biggest Little Wild West Show On Earth, The Story of Buckskin Ben Stalker's Family Wild West Show.* It was published in 1997. Her stories and columns have appeared in the *Hagerstown Exponent, AntiqueWeek* and the Indiana Historical Society magazine, *Traces of Indiana and Midwestern History.*

Carolyn Lafever is a graduate of Ball State University with a master's degree in music. She and her husband, Edward, are parents of four grown children and grandparents of six. Their home is on a farm in Dalton Township near Hagerstown.